中宮寺門跡
CHŪGŪJI IMPERIAL CONVENT

光村推古書院

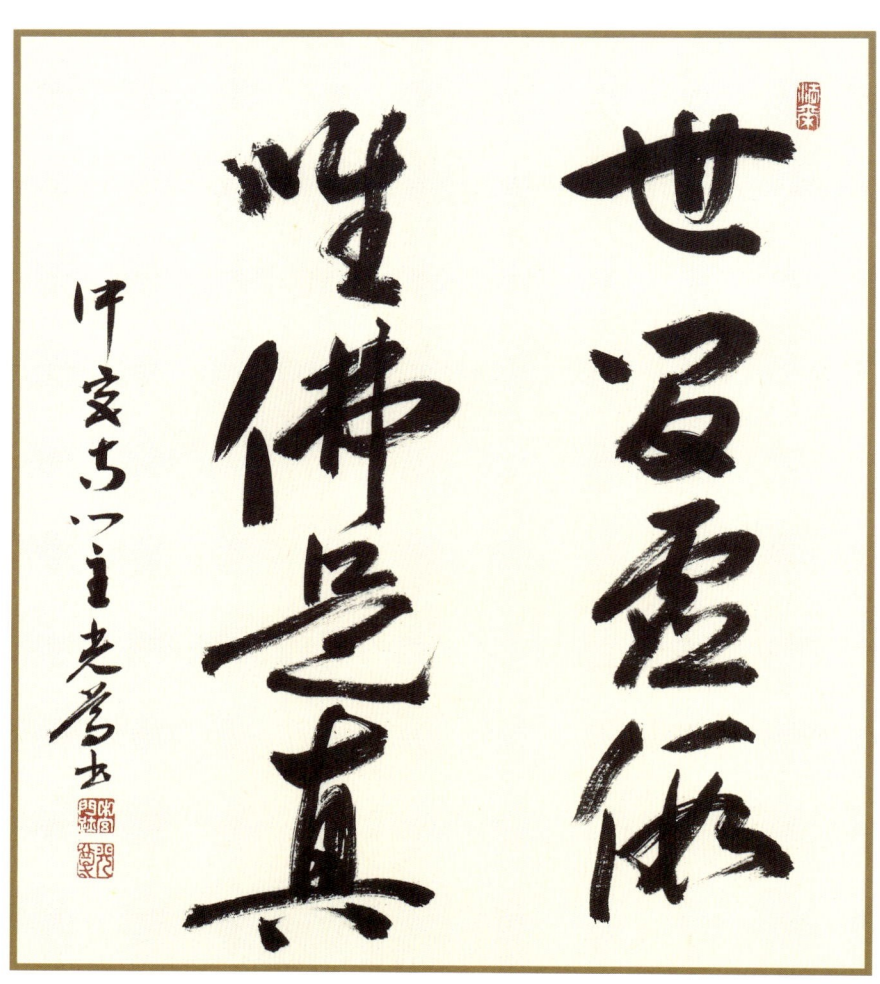

Calligraphy of the words of Prince Shōtoku by Chūgūji Abbess Hinonishi Kōson: "The world is empty; the only truth is Buddha."

ごあいさつ

「世間虚仮　唯仏是真」は、聖徳太子が常に仰せになったお言葉で、当中宮寺所蔵の国宝「天寿国曼荼羅繡帳」に刺繡されております。

「天寿国曼荼羅繡帳」は、聖徳太子崩御の後、お妃の橘大郎女が大層お嘆きになり、太子のおわす天寿国（極楽浄土）のありさまを想像なさり、東漢末賢・高麗加世溢・漢奴加己利に描かせ、それを宮中の采女達に刺繡させて出来上がったものです。

聖徳太子は、「和を以て貴しと為す」など憲法十七条でよく知られておりますように、この世を争いのない平和な世の中にしたいとのお考えであったことは、ご存じの通りです。

「世間虚仮」とは「諸行無常」と同じく、この世の中はとどまる処がなく、常に移り変わり、何物も実体のあるものはない。いつ崩れ去っても不思議ではない仮の姿、虚の姿であるということです。

「唯仏是真」は「唯、仏のみ是れ真実である」という、本当の自分探しの教えです。煩悩にがんじがらめの自分が、何のとらわれもなくなり、無我の境地、空に至った状態を申します。それこそが本当の自分であり、真実であり、これを見究めることの大切さを太子は仰せになっていらっしゃるのです。

本当の自分に気付き、天地草木、あらゆる人々や物に包まれ、支えられている自分、そして、選ばれて生かされている、一度しかない自分の人生を感謝して生きたいものです。太子のみ心、お言葉を有難く思い返し、このみ心が、広く皆様に伝わることを念じてやみません。

合掌

中宮寺門跡
日野西光尊

目　次

ごあいさつ　　　　　　　　　　　　　　　　　　　　　　　　　日野西光尊　3

■歴　史
中宮寺―女性たちが伝えつづけた太子の心　　　　　　　　久我なつみ　13

■修　復
ワールド・モニュメント財団より　　　　　　　　　　　ボニー・バーナム　36
尼門跡修復プロジェクトについて　　　　　　　　　　ヘンリー・エンジー　38
中宮寺表御殿の修復　　　　　　　　　　　　　　　　　　　金出ミチル　42

謝辞　　　　　　　　　　　　　　　　　　　　　　　　　　　　　　　　78

Contents

■HISTORY
History of Chūgūji　　　　　　　　　　　　　　　　　Catherine Ludvik　18

■RESTORATION
A Word from World Monuments Fund　　　　　　　　Bonnie Burnham　37
Japanese Imperial Buddhist Convents Projects　　　　　　Henry Tzu Ng　40
Restoration of the Chūgūji Royal Reception Suite　　　Michiru Kanade　43

Acknowledgements　　　　　　　　　　　　　　　　　　　　　　　　79

扉：天寿国繡帳（部分）　間人皇后の名前のある亀形

中宮寺の歴史

HISTORY OF CHŪGŪJI

国宝　菩薩半跏像　白鳳時代(7世紀)　高87.9cm
Pensive Bodhisattva

国宝　天寿国繡帳　飛鳥時代（622年銘）　88.8×82.7cm
Tenjukoku Shūchō Mandala

木造南無仏太子立像
鎌倉時代　像高67.8cm
Prince Shōtoku as child

木造摂政太子坐像
江戸時代　像高56.0cm
Prince Regent Shōtoku

重要文化財　聖皇曼荼羅　鎌倉時代　建長6年(1254)　163.5×117.0cm　法隆寺所蔵
Shōkō Mandala

中宮寺の歴史

HISTORY OF CHŪGŪJI

絹本著色伝信如比丘尼像　鎌倉時代　111.8×58.4cm
Nun Shinnyo

梨子地菊紋蒔絵書見台　江戸時代　総高57.8（箱台高10.9）×幅45.5×奥行27.3cm
Bookstand with imperial chrysanthemum-crest design

梨子地社景文蒔絵硯箱　江戸時代　総高4.5×幅21.4×奥行23.6cm
Writing box with landscape and shrine design

本堂

境内より(春)

境内より(夕方)

表門

中庭

表御殿と桃

境内より(春)、境内より(夕方)、中庭、表御殿と桃の4点は、日野西が撮影。

中宮寺―女性たちが伝えつづけた太子の心

　大阪と奈良をへだてる生駒山系の東麓の、斑鳩(いかるが)の野には聖徳太子ゆかりの寺々が甍(いらか)をならべ、「和をもって貴しとなす」と日本の礎(いしずえ)をさだめた、英雄の偉業を今に伝えている。
　太子の宮跡として名高い法隆寺、嫡子の山背大兄王(やましろのおおえのおう)が一族のために建てた法起寺、法輪寺。名刹が千古の歴史を誇るなか、唯一の尼寺である中宮寺は法隆寺の夢殿そばに、ひっそりと控えている。
　心安らぐ土色の油塀にかこまれた、夢殿をめぐる道をすすむと、果てに中宮寺の表門がみえてくる。松や椿、菴羅樹(あんらじゅ)の木立を抱えた寺域は、人を迎えてくつろがせるのに必要なだけの広さ。表御殿や阿弥陀堂、そして本尊の如意輪観世音菩薩をまもる新本堂と、いずれの建物もこぶりで、やさしい風情が漂っている。
　母穴穂部間人皇后(あなほべのはしひと)の菩提をとむらうため、太子の発願により創建されたというこの尼寺は、法隆寺に寄り添いながら、西に峻険な山容を、日出る東に、遠く飛鳥をみつめている。

　聖徳太子が活躍した7世紀初頭は、仏教文化が花開いた、飛鳥時代の全盛期であった。名がしめすとおり、宮城は飛鳥におかれていた。太子の父用明天皇、太子が摂政をつとめた推古女帝もしかりである。
　太子は政界の中枢にいながら、なぜ自身の宮を飛鳥ではなく、12キロ離れた斑鳩においたのだろう。
　私はそのことを、長年、疑問に思ってきた。
　聖徳太子が、日本の歴史に与えた影響ははかりしれない。彼の「和」の言葉は、日本人なら、全身に染みついている。それだけ身近に感じながら、太子の行動、挙措進退(きょそしんたい)は理解しづらい。斑鳩に宮をさだめたこと、編纂した『天皇紀(てんのうき)』で初めて天皇という言葉をもちいたとされ、女帝を時にしのぐ働きをしながら、彼自身は天皇にのぼっていないこと等々。「英雄にして英雄を知る」と、世に言う。太子の本意、その深甚なる思想を、

私たち凡人が識るのは不可能なのかと思いもする。幼少より抜群の才知をあらわして父帝に愛され、群臣に「未然の事を知る」と崇敬された。
　しかし足跡を語りつぐ斑鳩の地にたつと、不思議と、謎めいた生涯がわかる気がする。すくなくとも、近づける気がする。

　聖徳太子の祖父は、欽明天皇である。長きにわたって平和が保たれ、仏教が公伝し、飛鳥百年といわれる新時代の先頭をきった栄えの御世だった。太子の父の用明天皇、母の穴穂部間人皇后はともに欽明天皇を父とした、異母兄妹である。古代においては、母が違えば、兄妹の結婚が許されていた。
　父の母は堅塩媛、母の母は小姉君。権勢をふるった蘇我氏の娘たちだった。しかし姉妹ながら、運命は明暗を分け、堅塩媛の子たちは用明、推古と帝位に次々ついたのに、小姉君は追いやられた。彼女の子供たちは同じく欽明天皇を父としながら皇位継承争いに破れ、殺された。穴穂部皇子、宅部皇子、そして崇峻天皇…
　ただ一人生き残ったのが、聖徳太子の母だった。
　争いを燎原の火のように燃え広がらせたのは、太子の伯父、母の兄であった蘇我馬子である。
　「此の世をば我世とぞ思う」と詠った藤原氏に比される蘇我大臣の専横により、母は兄弟を亡くした。悲嘆に沈む母の姿を、聖徳太子は目に焼きつけて、成長した。
　さらに複雑なことに、蘇我馬子は太子の妻の父であった。憎い宿敵を、岳父と仰がねばならない。恩讐が断ち切るほかないほど縺れこじれた、蘇我大臣がのし歩く飛鳥を太子は離れて、斑鳩に移ったのである。摂政となってから9年目。いまだ政争の渦中に身をおきながらの、決断だった。
　今でも、斑鳩宮跡を歩くと、まるで隠里のような風情がある。
　難波の津への往還が盛んだった奈良街道が近いのに、へだてられた感じが漂う。すぐ北に、矢田丘陵を背負うせいだろう。斑鳩の甍の群れは、低い山に隠れ、人目を避けているかのようだ。

ここに宮をもった、太子の判断の的確さに、感嘆せざるをえない。東は野がひろがって、一朝事ある時は、飛鳥にすぐさま乗りこめる。狼煙が火急を告げれば、生駒山に逃げこめる。山系は霧氷がみられるほど高峻で、ひとたび樹海に身を沈めれば、探索はむつかしい。事実、太子没後、息の山背大兄王は蘇我氏の追討をここでかわそうとした。

　太子は斑鳩から、時々刻々かわっていく政治情勢をみつめ、最適の瞬間を逃さなかった。母の兄弟を惨殺した蘇我氏さえ時に操り、日本初の憲法ともいわれる十七条憲法を制定するなど、清新な政策を打ちだし成功させた。

　辣腕は、外交に、いかんなく発揮された。

　国の興亡をくりかえす中国大陸や、高句麗・新羅・百済が相争う朝鮮半島のいり組んだ国際情勢を、太子は、万里の波濤の彼方から見透かしていた。そして607年、隋へ正使を派遣した。

　このとき隋は、悲願とした高句麗征伐に苦慮して百済を味方に誘おうとしていた。さらに日本を引き入れたら、高句麗を囲いこめる。隋が日本の利用価値を意識しだした、絶好の機会を太子はとらえて、使者をおくったのだ。

　その国際感覚は、グローバルな現代こそ、刮目に値する。天空の鷲が野ウサギを狙うように、隋が周辺諸国をうかがうとき、太子は臆することなく、隋と敵対する高句麗と誼を通じつづけた。紙墨法伝授で知られる高句麗の僧曇徴を迎えいれ、さらに高句麗とは犬猿の仲の百済とも友好関係をたもつバランスのよさ。

　何より範とすべきは、新羅への対処だ。欽明天皇以来の懸案であった新羅出兵は、太子が摂政のとき中止となった。仏教信仰にもとづく平和主義を、太子は生涯にわたって、内政外交ともども、貫きとおした。

　そして朝鮮半島から伝わった仏教を、さらに奥の、中国に学んだ。知識と思索を深めて、国の基本を「一に曰く、和を以て貴しとし、二に曰く、篤く三宝を敬え。三宝とは仏法僧なり」と定め、仏教文化を花開かせた。

　偉人中の偉人、聖徳太子が命終を迎えたとき、一族の嘆き、哀しみは、どれほど深かっただろう。

中宮寺を訪れると、太子への深い思慕と崇敬が身に沁みて、感動せずにいられない。名高い「天寿国繡帳」をみると、その想いはとりわけ強くなる。

妃の橘大郎女が亡き太子の往生後を絵にしてしのびたいと願い、采女たちに命じて繡いあらわさせたものという。

太子との縁が確実な遺物として貴重で、国宝となっている。

長い時を経て傷みが激しいが、復元の努力と研究がすすんでいる。蓮華から化生する天人を僧俗の男女が礼拝するさまなどが描かれていて興味深いが、とりわけ注目すべきは、散りばめられた亀の姿だろう。もとは約100個あったと推定されており、各々の甲に四文字が刻まれ、全体で400字程度の銘文をなしている。現在は、太子の母の名「部間人公」などごく一部が読めるだけで、解読は困難をきわめる。

幸いなことに、聖徳太子の事跡を伝える典籍『上宮法王帝説』(成立不詳。推定奈良時代。現存最古の写本は平安時代中期)が398文字を拾遺している。しかし他の模本にみえる亀甲一つ分、つまり四文字を欠き、さらに「然」一字を別の二字にするなど、錯誤がある。

銘文自体も、前半は太子の家系を万葉仮名でしるし、後半は漢文と、表記が複雑で、解釈に異説がある。

だが、そこに、誰もが誤らずに読める、八文字がある。

「世間虚仮　唯仏是真」

太子が常に口にしていたという、有名なこの言葉は、驚くべきことに、「天寿国繡帳」に縫いこまれていたのだ。

聖徳太子の没後、蘇我氏により、一族は滅亡した。中宮寺も時代の波に翻弄された。

創建は現在地より半キロ東であったことが発掘調査により確かめられているが、それがいつ荒廃し、いつ法隆寺夢殿そばに移ったか、定かではない。

由緒ある尼寺を再興した、伝説的な女傑があらわれたのは、鎌倉時代だ。興福寺の学僧の娘で、信如尼という。彼女は、行方不明といわれて

いた「天寿国繡帳」の探索にのりだした。粘り強い努力により、見事、法隆寺の宝庫綱封蔵に秘蔵されていた繡帳を世に知らしめた。文永11年の出来事という。

信如尼は朝廷に働きかけ、レプリカを作った。そして繡帳が新たに甦ったとき、亀山上皇の臨席により、盛大に法会をもよおした。

なぜこんな大事業を、一尼僧がなしえたのか。

不思議に思えるが、歴史をひもとくと、気づくことがある。文永年間というと、フビライの国書が到来し、人々が恐れおののいていたときだ。信如尼が繡帳を発見したのは文永11年。まさにその年、蒙古が大軍をもって襲来したのである。国をあげて敵国降伏を祈願し、神風により事なきをえた直後、繡帳は京に運ばれていった。朝廷は復活に大いに力を貸した。未曽有の国難が、影響していないはずがない。

かくして中宮寺は寺勢をとりもどし、「天寿国繡帳」を寺宝として護りぬいていく。戦国武将が覇権を争った天文年間には、皇女が住持するようになった。宮家から尼門跡をむかえる、いわゆる尼門跡寺院として確立したのは江戸時代である。したがって旧地の礎石は四天王寺式伽藍配置をしめすが、今の建造物は江戸時代の寺院様式をみせる。

このたび修復された迎賓用の表御殿も江戸時代につくられたもの。寺院ゆえ決して華美ではないが、隅々まで心がつくされて、美しい。尼門跡の御座所だった上段の間は、瑞鳥や花の折枝を散りばめた金地の襖絵にかこまれ、遙か遠い飛鳥時代から続いた皇統をしのばせる。

千年を超す長い歳月、命脈をたもったこの寺院が、今、日本の内外から力強い支援をうけるのは、世界に開かれた聖徳太子の心を受け継いだからこそだろう。

如意輪観世音菩薩は両腕をゆるやかに開き、人々の苦悩を受け止めながら、穏やかに微笑んでいる。

久我なつみ

主要参考文献
『聖徳太子』坂本太郎　吉川弘文館（1979年）
『天寿国繡帳の研究』大橋一章　吉川弘文館（1995年）

HISTORY OF CHŪGŪJI

INTRODUCTION

Chūgūji is an Imperial Buddhist Convent in the Ikaruga area of Nara, located on the northeast side of the great Hōryūji monastery's Eastern Precinct (Tōin Garan), just steps from Hōryūji's famous Dream Hall (Yumedono). As Japan's oldest nunnery, with a history of almost 1400 years, Chūgūji enshrines images of great renown designated as National Treasures, and it houses a Royal Reception Suite (Omote Goten) certified as a Nationally Registered Cultural Property. The Imperial Convent preserves a religious and cultural heritage highlighted especially during three periods in its long history: the era of its establishment in the residence of Empress Hashihito in the early part of the 7th century, its restoration by the extraordinary nun Shinnyo in the late 13th century, and its official designation as an Imperial Convent when Princess Jikakuin, followed by other royal women, was made abbess in the second quarter of the 16th century.

Aerial view (old photo)

ORIGINS OF CHŪGŪJI

Chūgūji (Temple Palace of the Imperial Consort) was originally the palace-residence of Empress Anahobe no Hashihito (?–621), mother of Japan's most famous early advocate of Buddhism, Prince Shōtoku (Prince Umayado, 574–622), and its establishment as a convent has been attributed either to the Empress herself or to the Prince. Some narratives from the 10th century onwards recount that Prince Shōtoku converted her residence into a nunnery when his mother passed away in 621, while other sources, in contrast, tell us that Empress Hashihito erected Chūgūji's pagoda in 587, following the death of her spouse Emperor Yōmei.

Prince Regent Shōtoku, Edo period

Excavated roof tile, 7th c.

Archaeological excavations at Chūgūji's original site, some five hundred meters east of its present location, however, indicate that neither of these accounts may be accurate. An analysis of surviving roof tiles from the remains of the main hall of worship (Golden Hall) and the pagoda, aligned on a north-south axis, suggests that the nunnery was probably built during the late 620s, some years after the death of both the Prince and his mother.

Descendants of Prince Shōtoku, namely his eldest son Prince Yamashiro and his daughters Tsukishine and Kataoka, most likely played prominent roles in the establishment of Chūgūji as a convent memorializing and deifying their father, and forming a pair with the great

Relics excavated from the pagoda's foundation stone, 7th c.

monastery Hōryūji founded by Prince Shōtoku.

Two of Chūgūji's precious treasures, both dating from the 7th century and both associated with Prince Shōtoku, are especially well known: its main image, a wooden statue worshipped by the convent as the Bodhisattva Nyoirin Kannon, and the embroidered Tenjukoku Shūchō Mandala.

PENSIVE BODHISATTVA

Chūgūji's principal image was produced during the second half of the 7th century and is designated a National Treasure. The pensive Bodhisattva is seated, with right ankle resting across left knee, the elegantly curved finger of the right hand delicately touching the right cheek. The slender, yet broad-shouldered youthful figure wears only a lower garment, which drapes amply over the round seat in gently cascading lines, lending a striking contrast to the smooth bare torso. The two-knobbed hairstyle, a common hairdo for Chinese, Tang-period youth, complements the human-like, intimate quality of the facial expression, with eyes half-closed and a slight inward smile. The richly intricate halo on a wooden pole behind the statue, moreover, is effectively offset by the unassuming simplicity of the upper body. Seven small seated Buddhas are carved on the aureole's quivering flame pattern, encircling floral and other bands around a central lotus flower. The remarkable beauty of Chūgūji's gentle Bodhisattva in an intimately contemplative mood is manifestly displayed from the viewer's every angle.

Pensive Bodhisattva, 7th c.

The deity's magnificent, almost life-size (ht. 87.9 cm) sculpture is made of fragrant camphorwood, impervious to insects, which was the preferred wood for statuary in the 7th century. Only the pole that supports the halo is made of Japanese cypress. Due to defects in the camphorwood, the sculptor carved the Bodhisattva and his pedestal from at least twenty-four different pieces, which were joined with wooden pegs and nails. The statue was then painted deep red and covered with a very thin coating of lacquer, resulting in a shiny finish. Darkened over time, the sculpture today appears almost black, as if made of metal.

Pensive Bodhisattva, 7th c.

Lastly, the majestic figure probably also wore a metal crown and other resplendent bodily ornaments, and might additionally have been gilded.

There are similar images of pensive Bodhisattvas throughout Asia, which are identified either as Prince Siddhārtha, or as the Buddha of the future Maitreya (Jp. Miroku), or as the Bodhisattva Avalokiteśvara (Jp. Kannon). Contemplative figures representing Maitreya arose in the Korean peninsula in the 6th century, at a time when young aristocratic warriors of the Hwarang Order of Silla were associated with this particular Bodhisattva. The Korean cult of Maitreya played a prominent role in the introduction of Buddhist images to Japan, where statues of this exceedingly handsome, introspective princely deity, with one leg crossed over the other, were both imported and extensively produced. It is most likely that Chūgūji's sculpture was also originally intended as a depiction of the pensive Maitreya, enshrined at the convent in commemoration of Prince Shōtoku.

By the 13th century, however, Chūgūji's pensive image was identified as Guze (World Savior) Kannon, reflecting growing faith in both the Bodhisattva and in Prince Shōtoku as his incarnation. Then, through the pervasive influence of esoteric Shingon Buddhism, where Nyoirin (Wish-fulfilling Jewel and Wheel) Kannon gained popularity, the convent's statue was in turn identified as Nyoirin Kannon, and continues to be worshipped as such today.

TENJUKOKU SHŪCHŌ MANDALA

The other greatly famed Chūgūji treasure is Japan's oldest embroidery, the Tenjukoku Shūchō Mandala (Embroidered Curtain Mandala of the 'Heavenly Land of Long Life'), which has been the subject of ceaseless, intensive study and speculation. Consisting of two groups of embroidered textile fragments made 650 years apart and mounted arbitrarily on a square support fabric (88.8×82.7 cm), this fascinating piece is one of Japan's great mysteries.

Tenjukoku Shūchō Mandala, 622

The first set of fragments are the remains of two embroidered curtains (shūchō) depicting the 'Heavenly Land of Long Life' (Tenjukoku), which were produced some time after the death of Prince Shōtoku and his mother in the early 620s. The second set are the remains of an exact replica of the original Tenjukoku Shūchō, this one called the Tenjukoku Mandala, made in 1275 at the time of the restoration of Chūgūji. The original was already in lamentable condition in the 13th century, and then the two sets were apparently damaged in fires at Chūgūji in 1309 and 1311. Not surprisingly, by 1731 both embroideries

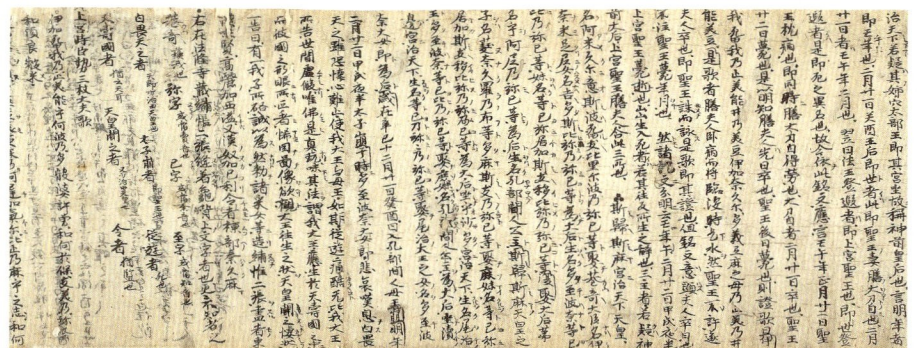

Tenjukoku Shūchō Mandala inscription in the *Jōgū Shōtoku hōō teisetsu*, 11th c., Chion'in

were already in pieces, and so in the late 18th century their fragments were pasted on a silk support fabric, and made into a hanging scroll (Tenjukoku Shūchō Mandala). White-silk faces with painted black features were added, and in 1919 the priceless hanging scroll was framed and placed in a glass shrine. Then, in 1952 the Tenjukoku Shūchō Mandala was designated a National Treasure, and finally, in 1982, due to its inestimable value it was moved to the Nara National Museum for safekeeping, and replaced at the convent by a replica.

Fortunately, the embroidered curtains were inscribed, as attested by the turtles with four characters on each shell found on the surviving fragments. There are twenty-five extant characters in total, preserved not just on the Tenjukoku Shūchō Mandala itself, but also on other fragments originally at nearby Hōryūji, which eventually ended up in the Shōsōin repository of the great Tōdaiji monastery of Nara. Although only five turtles remain (four in the Mandala and one in the Shōsōin), there were apparently one hundred of them, and the inscription of 398 characters (two missing characters) can be found in a mid-Heian period (794–1185) text entitled *Jōgū Shōtoku hōō teisetsu*. Decoding the turtle shell inscription, however, was no small feat even

Turtle in Tenjukoku Shūchō Mandala

in the 13th century, when the curtains were rediscovered at the outset of Chūgūji's revival. At the time, this painstaking task involved also the assistance of a priest from a shrine controlled by the Urabe clan, who, most interestingly, happened to be specialists in turtle-shell divination. The embroidered characters describe the genealogy of Prince Shōtoku and his consort Lady Tachibana, and recount the circumstances under which the curtains were originally produced: after Empress Anahobe no Hashihito passed away in 621 and was closely followed in death by her son Prince Shōtoku in 622, grieving Lady Tachibana expressed a wish to see her spouse in Tenjukoku. Ladies at the court were therefore put to work embroidering curtains with what is believed to be an image of the heavenly land inhabited by the Prince.

Shōtoku's post-mortem world identified in the inscription as Tenjukoku, however, remains an unresolved enigma, interpreted variously as the paradise of one of several different Buddhas, most often Amida's Western Pure Land; an exotic place, such as India; sites associated with Chinese beliefs, like Mt. Penglai (Jp. Hōrai), the legendary island-mountain of the immortals; and the afterlife world. Motifs on the surviving fragments are closely related to what appears in 5th- to 6th-century Chinese and Korean funerary monuments, and display pre-Buddhist afterlife iconography overlapping with specifically Buddhist subjects. One reconstruction of the curtains locates the reborn Prince Shōtoku on a lotus at the center of one panel and the Buddha of Tenjukoku on the other panel, with a lotus pond extending across the bottom. The pair of curtains, it has been suggested, may have been sewn together, and hung around the Prince's bed at Lady Tachibana's palace. Another interpretation proposes that the curtains, an important part of funerary paraphernalia in East Asia, were produced as a visual record of the funerary rituals performed for the Prince and his mother, and might have been intended for hanging along the walls of their burial chamber.

The Tenjukoku Shūchō then inexplicably ended up in a trunk at nearby Hōryūji, seemingly forgotten, with the exception of the embroidery's inscription noted in the above-mentioned mid-Heian period text. In the next episode of the mysterious curtains, however, they were rediscovered by the enterprising 13th-century nun Shinnyo, amidst her efforts to restore Chūgūji.

Little is known of the convent's history in the intervening years until the arrival of Shinnyo (1211–?) on the scene. Throughout the 8th to the 11th century, the convent's residents seem to have been mostly a small number of itinerant nuns and retired court ladies who had gathered in Nara, devoting themselves to a life of courtly pursuits and prayer. The convent's main hall and pagoda are thought to be depicted on a folding screen from the year 1069, which represents the legendary life of Prince Shōtoku (Shōtoku Taishi eden byōbu). During the 12th century, the nunnery was managed by the Hōryūji monastery, which supervised renovations and repairs to the convent's main hall and pagoda. By the mid-13th century, however, Chūgūji had fallen into a deplorable state of neglect, as attested by Shinnyo: she describes pine trees taking root among the roof tiles, temple-fences being used to dry laundry, and the altar infested with lizards and frogs. Evidently, it was high time for a revival, and none was more equal to the task than the dynamic nun herself.

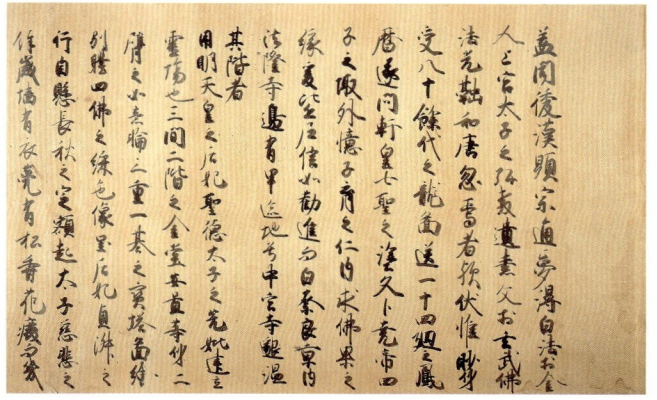

Nun Shinnyo's Petition (*Ama Shinnyo Ganmon*) for Chūgūji, describing the convent's deplorable state, 1281

NUN SHINNYO

Shinnyo's father was a scholar-priest of the Nara monastery Kōfukuji, who by all accounts was a poor and fallen cleric, having taken a wife. His writings, however, provided for his daughter's livelihood, as she supported herself by allowing monks to read her father's works in exchange for payment. Having been educated by a scholar-priest, Shinnyo herself was well trained in Buddhist doctrinal texts, and displayed considerable learning, including the necessary ability to read Chinese. She was ordained sometime between 1244 and 1249, and trained at Hokkeji, the center of a nuns' revival movement that at the time was about to take momentum, so much so that by the late 1200s the convent had apparently

Nun Shinnyo (may originally have been produced as a painting of monk Rāhula, son of the Buddha), Kamakura period

over five hundred nuns in residence. Education at Hokkeji prepared these women to take positions as abbesses of smaller nunneries, and Shinnyo herself went on to found Shōbōji, before coming to Chūgūji in 1262. Her restoration work at Chūgūji, to which she was drawn through her devotion to Prince Shōtoku, began when she was in her early fifties and extended over at least two decades.

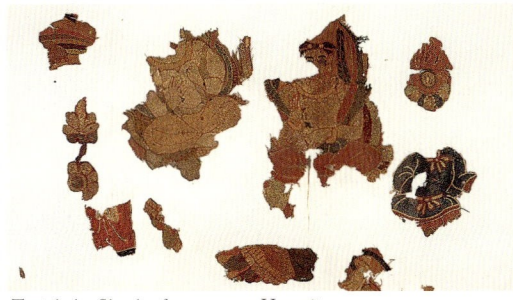

Tenjukoku Shūchō fragments at Hōryūji

Shinnyo's initial efforts were centered on the recovery of the already legendary Tenjukoku embroidered curtains, a story dramatically recounted in fundraising campaigns and in popular narratives of her life. Guided by a dream, she requested to search for the curtains at Hōryūji. Although at first refused, when a thief broke into the monastery's treasury, a group, which Shinnyo joined, went in to inventory the temple's valuable items. On this occasion, in 1274, she discovered the precious curtains disintegrating in a trunk, and, perhaps on account of their pitiful condition, the nun obtained permission to remove them from the monastery. Resourceful Shinnyo then took the embroidery to Kyoto, where she found people able to assist her in deciphering the text on the turtle shells. Mission accomplished, the spirited nun was then ready to take the damaged curtains on tour, using them as a prop to raise interest and funds for the Chūgūji revival, focusing primarily on elite women with ties to the court. Shinnyo achieved one of her aims in 1275, when she succeeded in having an exact replica of the Tenjukoku embroidery produced.

The purported motivation for the recovery of the curtains was to find out the death date of Empress Hashihito, which appears in the turtle shell inscription, so that commemorative services for her could be held. At this time, ample literature was produced to bring the Empress out of the shadow of the cult of Prince Shōtoku, by resurrecting her as the female founder and patron deity of Chūgūji, as an incarnation of the Buddha Amida, and as the Buddha of the Tenjukoku paradise depicted on the treasured curtains. Accordingly, the Tenjukoku Shūchō was treated as a mandala relic of the Empress, serving as documentary and visual evidence to legitimate Chūgūji's history and to spearhead its revival under the leadership of Shinnyo.

EMPRESS HASHIHITO DEIFIED

Heian-period legendary accounts of Prince Shōtoku depict Empress Hashihito as a passive receptacle, defiled by virtue of her gender, receiving in her womb the Prince as an incarnation of the Bodhisattva Kannon. He appears to her in a dream, and, following a brief exchange, leaps into her mouth, as she awakens pregnant. From about the mid-11th century, however, the Prince's identification with Kannon was configured into an Amida triad, by rendering his mother into the Buddha Amida and his consort Kashiwade Bunin into the Bodhisattva Seishi, and connecting this equation with the purported burial of the three in the same tomb, interpreted as 'the Amida triad in the tomb with three bodies.'

The Shōkō (Eminent Prince) Mandala (1254), designed in the mid-13th century by the monk Kenshin as part of the movement to revive the Shōtoku cult at Hōryūji, depicts this version of the Amida triad, encircled by other figures connected with the Prince, including his relatives, his associates, and his various incarnations. Empress Hashihito as Amida appears in the center of this mandala, represented in Heian-period robes, her hair cropped like a partially tonsured aristocratic nun. Shōtoku as Kannon is seated to her left, and his consort Kashiwade as Seishi sits to her right. Although the Empress takes center stage, the focus is intended to be on Shōtoku, to whom all the figures in the painting are related and to whom they turn their gaze.

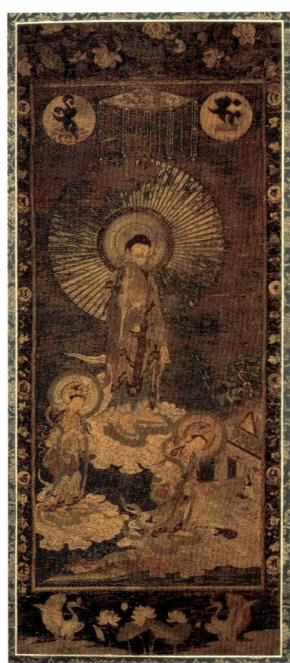

Descent of Amida triad, 14th c., silk embroidery

Shōkō Mandala, 1254, Hōryūji

Building on the association of Empress Hashihito with Amida and shifting worship from Prince Shōtoku to his mother, subsequent 13th-century Chūgūji literature expanded her role in a newly developed hagiography, making Hashihito, like Amida, the dominant figure in the triad. Following her death, the *Shōtoku Taishi denki* (1274) recounts, she appears to her grieving son Shōtoku, telling him that she will remain in this world to help those with karmic ties to her, and that she will create a Tenjukoku paradise within the defiled world, destined for beings whose karmic burdens prevent them from entering Amida's Western Pure Land. When she manifests her newly founded paradise to her son, the Prince draws the image of Tenjukoku, on the basis of which court ladies then embroider the famed Tenjukoku curtains.

Empress Hashihito's Tenjukoku is not only a kind of satellite paradise to Amida's Western Pure Land, more accessible by virtue of its location in this polluted world itself, but it too has a satellite of its own, Chūgūji. Serving as an approach to Tenjukoku, the Empress's earthly dwelling leads directly to her heavenly abode. Even one pilgrimage to Chūgūji, says the 13th-century *Chūgūji engi*, will result in birth in Tenjukoku.

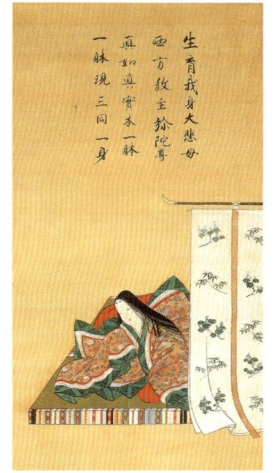

Empress Hashihito, 18th c.

If we consider, furthermore, the depiction of Empress Hashihito in either the above mentioned 1254 Shōkō Mandala of Hōryūji or in an 18th-century hanging scroll belonging to Chūgūji, it is noteworthy, although not unusual, that an Asuka-period (552–645) woman is represented anachronistically in centuries-later Heian-period (794–1185) robes. Moreover, as already remarked, her hairstyle, displaying locks cut shoulder-length in the front, reveals that she is a partially ordained aristocratic nun. From the 11th century onwards, private ordination, involving the reception of some form of the precepts and the cutting of a token of hair, became a regular, lavishly performed practice among both elite men and women. Having ceremonially affirmed their dedication to Buddhism, aristocratic ladies could thereby become 'lay nuns,' in contrast with full-fledged monastics. Therefore, when Shinnyo sought to attract the support of such, perhaps less affluent, Kamakura-period (1185–1333) court women, the representation of Empress Hashihito as both one of them, as well as an idealized Heian-style empress of the former glory days of the court, might have served well as an appealing lay model of Buddhist practice and as an attractive courtly lineage with which to be affiliated. Despite the Buddhist perception of the insurmountable karmic impediments of the female body, Chūgūji's founder and patron deity, herself a woman, besides providing a model and a lineage, also offered the comforting promise of the Tenjukoku paradise awaiting them. This message and appeal, furthermore, was delivered to them through the powerful spiritual descendant of the Empress, the well educated, dynamic, fearless nun Shinnyo, who embodied the paragon of female monasticism.

Shinnyo's successful campaign led to the reconstruction and expansion of Chūgūji on the basis of the nunnery's early records, and the restoration was brought to completion in 1281. Unfortunately, thirty years later, the living quarters were twice destroyed by fire, once in 1309 and again in 1311. Then, little is known about Chūgūji until the fundraising of 1522–1540, suggesting that the nunnery may once more have gone through a period of some decline between the 14th and the 15th century.

IMPERIAL CONVENT

The convent entered the third important phase of its history when Prince Fushimi no miya's daughter, Princess Jikakuin, joined the nunnery as the nun Sonchi and became its abbess (1532–1554). Although Chūgūji had had imperial connections since its very founding in the 620s, it was only from the 16th century that its successive abbesses began systematically to be drawn from imperial and aristocratic lines, officially rendering the nunnery into an 'imperial' convent. A further notable 16th-century development was Chūgūji's move about five hundred meters westwards, to its present location to the northeast corner of Hōryūji's Eastern Precinct.

Writing box with landscape and shrine design, 19th c.

Bookstand with imperial chrysanthemum-crest design, 19th c.

Construction and repairs took place at Chūgūji during the abbacy of Princess-nun Sonchi in the mid-16th century, then in the early 17th century, and again in the Genroku era (1688–1704). Finally, around 1696, the priory's identity as an Imperial Convent was architecturally completed, when the characteristic feature of imperial nunneries was added to its grounds: the Royal Reception Suite known as Omote Goten. In this lavishly decorated apartment, giving the nunnery the accoutrements of a temple palace, the princess-abbesses received royal guests. As daughters of Japan's highest ranking nobility, these young women entered Chūgūji and other imperial convents with every intention of maintaining, alongside their spiritual practice, their former lifestyle and cultural pursuits, including the cultivation of poetry, music, calligraphy, and painting. Arriving with all their wealth in tow, they brought with them everything from furnishings, garments, and books, to secular and

Lunch boxes, 19th c.

Biwa (lute), 19th c.

Powdered tea container with imperial chrysanthemum-crest design, 19th c.

religious scrolls, paintings, screens, lacquerware, as well as utensils for tea ceremony and flower arrangement. Completing the picture, in order that these noble-born abbesses could also hold court, adjustment to nunnery architecture was made through the addition of the Omote Goten.

Chūgūji's Royal Reception Suite consists of six tatami-mat rooms, ranging from three to eight mats each, divided by way of exquisitely painted sliding doors (fusuma). The most important of the rooms is the Jōdan no ma or Upper Level Chamber, elevated 'a step higher' (jōdan) than the suite's general flooring, and including a dais intended as the seat for the topmost ranking person, in this case the convent's princess-abbess, placed in front of a wide alcove (ōdoko), adjacent to a smaller, side alcove (wakidoko). This magnificent chamber is profusely decorated all around with beautiful wall and sliding-door paintings of flowers and phoenix birds in flight, set against a resplendent gold background, and surmounted with a coffered ceiling.

By the early 18th century, Chūgūji, like several other imperial convents, was aptly designated as a Nuns' Palace (Bikuni Gosho), and identified as the Ikaruga Palace (Ikaruga Gosho) after the name of the area. In its dedication to cultural arts, moreover, from the time of Princess-abbess Sonchin Eijo (1749–1776), the nunnery developed its own tea ceremony and flower arrangement schools, known respectively as Kōgetsu Goryū and

Princess-abbess Sonchin Eijo (Jigen'in no miya), 18th c.

Ikaruga Goryū, which remain active to this day.

Japan's imperial convent system reached its culmination under Tokugawa patronage in the early 19th century, when there were at least thirty imperial convents. In the Meiji Restoration of 1868, however, as Shinto ideology was adopted by the State, and Buddhism entered a period of persecution, half of the imperial convents were forcibly disbanded. With government decrees that removed imperial support from Buddhist institutions, princesses and other aristocratic women were forbidden to join Buddhist nunneries, the designation Nuns' Palace was abolished, buildings deteriorated, and the flowering of imperial convents came to an abrupt end. Chūgūji, however, managed to survive, and although its abbesses did not come from the imperial family anymore, its official status as a Bikuni Gosho was revived in 1888, and then in 1941 it was granted the designation of Ama Monzeki (Imperial Convent).

Altar cloth with wisteria and Japanese cypress fan designs, 1829

Fortunately, with time the winds of change facilitated major restorations at the nunnery in the early 20th century. As the main worship hall (Kannondō), constructed in 1690, was deemed unsafe to house the convent's precious image of the pensive Bodhisattva, in 1965 the old structure was moved to Gobōjakujōin temple on Mt. Kōya, while work began on a risk-free fire-proof building. Thanks to funds raised by Prince Takamatsu, the brother of the then-reigning Emperor Shōwa, and his wife Princess Takamatsu, a new Kannondō of reinforced concrete was completed in 1968. Ties with the imperial family were evidently maintained, and to this day Chūgūji continues to receive periodic visits from the Imperial Household.

In 1995, however, the convent's magnificent Royal Reception Suite sustained considerable damage in the devastating Kobe Earthquake. The

Banner with bamboo blind and chrysanthemum designs, 1806

restoration of the Omote Goten, completed in October 2008 and described in the second part of this book, was made possible through the gracious support of the World Monuments Fund of New York, as well as through the awareness- and fund-raising efforts of Chūgūji's current abbess Hinonishi Kōson and of numerous people throughout the country. In 2006, the Royal Reception Suite was certified as a Nationally Registered Cultural Property, and in December 2008, for the first time ever, the general public was allowed to view the Omote Goten, now exquisitely restored.

The last half-century of preservation activities at Chūgūji have taken place under the leadership of the current abbess Hinonishi Kōson, who entered the convent in 1960. She had been a kindegarten teacher, when she was approached by her great aunt, herself an Imperial Abbess (Monzeki), proposing that her grandniece would be a suitable candidate to head an imperial nunnery. Fully ordained in 1961, Hinonishi then became Chūgūji's Imperial Abbess in 1964. For almost fifty years, she has led a remarkably full life, rising everyday at dawn, and, following two hours of morning worship, energetically engaging in a long day filled with activity. Besides the convent's calendar of religious ceremonies and office work, the abbess presides over events related to Chūgūji's tea ceremony and flower arrangement schools, conducts meetings with worshippers, runs a women's circle, leads a zazen meditation group, gives personal consultations, and much more. Preserving the legacy of Japan's imperial nunneries, the life of Chūgūji's abbess has been one of cultural responsibility and dynamic activity.

Catherine Ludvik

SELECTED ENGLISH SOURCES AND RECOMMENDED READINGS

COMO, Michael
    2008   Of Temples, Horses, and Tombs: Hōryūji and Chūgūji in Heian and Early Kamakura Japan. In *Hōryūji Reconsidered*, ed. Dorothy C. Wong. Newcastle, U.K.: Cambridge Scholars Publishing, pp. 263–288.

GUTH, Christine M. E.
    1988   The Pensive Prince of Chūgūji: Maitreya Cult and Image in Seventh-century Japan. In *Maitreya, the Future Buddha*, ed. Alan Sponberg and Helen Hardacre. Cambridge: Cambridge University Press, pp. 191–213.

LEE, Junghee
    1993   The Origins and Development of the Pensive Bodhisattva Images of Asia. *Artibus Asiae* 53: 3/4, pp. 311–357.

MEEKS, Lori R.
    2007   In Her Likeness: Female Divinity and Leadership at Medieval Chūgūji. *Japanese Journal of Religious Studies* 34:2, pp. 351–392.
    2008   Chūgūji and Female Monasticism in the Age of Shōtoku. In *Hōryūji Reconsidered*, ed. Dorothy C. Wong. Newcastle, U.K.: Cambridge Scholars Publishing, pp. 237–262.

MORAN, Sherwood F.
    1958   The Statue of Miroku Bosatsu of Chūgūji: A Detailed Study. *Artibus Asiae* 21: 3/4, pp. 179–203.

PRADEL, Chari
    2004   The Tenjukoku Shūchō Mandara: Reconstruction of the Iconography and Ritual Context. In *Images in Asian Religions: Texts and Contexts*, ed. Phyllis Granoff and Koichi Shinohara. Vancouver: UBC Press, pp. 257–289.
    2008   Shōkō Mandara and the Cult of Prince Shōtoku in the Kamakura Period. *Artibus Asiae* 68:2. (Forthcoming 2009)

ワールド・モニュメント財団より

ボニー・バーナム　　ワールド・モニュメント財団 理事長

　今から10年ほど前になりますが、中世日本研究所のバーバラ・ルーシュ所長が、私どものニューヨーク本部を訪問されました。研究所の活動を始め、日本には大変貴重な尼門跡寺院というものがあること、そしてそれは1000年以上の歴史を持ち、宝石箱のように美しいが、速やかな修復の必要性があることなどを、それは熱心に話されました。そして2001年、私自身も尼門跡寺院を訪問させて頂きました。歴史的に重要な建造物の損傷が進んでいることを目のあたりにし、それ以来、私どもは何とかして、後世のために保存していかなければならないと考えました。

　尼門跡修復のプロジェクトは、ワールド・モニュメント財団が日本で行う初めての、そして一番大きなプロジェクトです。日本のように文化遺産を大切にされる国で活動させて頂くことは、私どもにとっても大変、名誉なことと考えております。

　ワールド・モニュメント財団は、世界各国でそれぞれの地域の方々と協力関係を築いて活動していますが、中宮寺門跡の修復の支援者として、まずフリーマン財団が最初に支援を快諾して下さいました。この財団は大変親日的であり、日本の歴史、伝統、文化に大変理解をお持ちです。そして、ティファニー財団は技術を重んじ、最も高いレベルの日本の伝統技術をつぎ込むために充分な支援をして下さいました。ロバート・ウィルソン財団の世界遺産保護プランは、マッチングファンドの概念のもと、より多くの日本の支援者の方から支援頂けるようにご協力下さいました。ワールド・モニュメント財団は、中宮寺門跡の歴史と未来を憂慮する多くの方々と一緒に、このプロジェクトを推進できたことを大変誇りに思っております。今回のプロジェクトで、皆様の関心が、このすばらしい表御殿という場所に及ぶだけでなく、あらためて多くの尼僧様たちが護り継がれてきたことにも及ぶことを願っております。

A Word from World Monuments Fund

Bonnie Burnham, President, World Monuments Fund

Professor Barbara Ruch first visited my office in New York almost ten years ago, to tell us about the Institute for Medieval Japanese Studies and her discovery of the extraordinary imperial Buddhist convents, with their jewel box like beauty and thousand-year history and their restoration needs. In 2001, I visited the convents and was immensely impressed both by the importance and the fragility of these distinguished institutions. From that time, we wanted to find a way to help preserve them for the future.

Preserving the imperial Buddhist convents became the first conservation project that the World Monuments Fund (WMF) undertook in Japan and it is still our largest commitment in Japan. It is a great privilege to be working here, in a country that has such deep appreciation for its heritage.

WMF works with partners internationally and at the local level and are fortunate to have as partners for the restoration of Chūgūji Imperial Convent, the Freeman Foundation, which has a deep respect and appreciation for Japan, its history, traditions, and culture, and which provided the initial funding for Chūgūji; to The Tiffany & Co. Foundation, for its support of the highest levels of traditional Japanese craftsmanship that were employed at Chūgūji; and to the Robert W. Wilson Challenge to Conserve our Heritage, which allowed WMF to offer matching funds that helped attract supporters from throughout Japan. The World Monuments Fund is proud to be a part of the growing number of people who care about the history—and the future—of Chūgūji Imperial Convent. We hope this project calls attention not only to these extraordinary places but to the exceptional women who devote their lives to them.

尼門跡修復プロジェクトについて

ヘンリー・エンジー　　ワールド・モニュメント財団 副理事長

　ワールド・モニュメント財団（WMF）は40年以上にわたり、90ヶ国以上で活動をしてまいりました。その中でも奈良・中宮寺門跡の修復プロジェクトはワールド・モニュメント財団が日本で携わった、最も大きなプロジェクトと言えます。ここでは、当財団の、このプロジェクトとの関わりと、私どもの世界での活動の一端をご説明できればと思います。

　ワールド・モニュメント財団は世界で最も大きな歴史的建造物の保存に努めている民間組織で、世界中で500以上の歴史的建造物をまもるために活動してきました。その中の大変有名な所では、カンボジアのアンコールワット遺跡や、フランス、ベルサイユのマリーアントワネットの劇場があります。また、あまり知られてはいないものの、重要な文化財も修復してまいりました。当財団では、政治や社会、また経済的な状況の違った色々な国で活動してきました。国毎に経済的な事情は異なっており、アフリカでも活動すれば、アメリカやイギリスでも支援活動を行ってまいりました。長年の間に気付きましたことはどの国も、経済状況に関わらず、また、文化遺産を充分に守っている国であっても、民間の人たちや民間の組織の役割は常にあるということです。

　ワールド・モニュメント財団は三つの観点から支援を行っております。まずは経済的な支援です。あるいは地域からの支援を得られるような協力的な共同体制をとることもあります。このような助成システムのおかげで、中宮寺の修復プロジェクトでは多くの支援を得られまして、私どもが提供するWMF／ウィルソン・チャレンジ助成金を拠出させていただきました。

　また、技術的な支援を行うケースもあり、構造的な支援やデザイン・意匠について、そして同じような問題を抱える建造物に対し、支援をさしのべることで、そのモデルケースとなれるように支援をしております。中宮寺のプロジェクトも最新の耐震調査を行い、建物としての安全性を診断し、解決策として屋根加重を軽減する方策をとりました。そして、あらたに防火用に空気管と防災装置を設置しました。室内の障壁画の修復工事も大規模修復のモデルケースと言えると思います。

ワールド・モニュメント財団は啓蒙することと、その財源となるものを提供することによって、歴史的地域への支援のお手伝いをいたします。WMFが民間の独立した建造物保存のための組織として、中宮寺門跡のようなプロジェクトに参加することにより、皆様の関心を募ることができ、結果として国内の支援がひろがることにつながります。地域の方々が世界遺産に匹敵するような価値あるものが自分たちの地域にあることに気付きます。尼門跡寺院の修復プロジェクトは、私どもWMFの事業のなかでも、特別の位置づけをしめております。WMFは世界でも有数の建造物の修復を手がけてまいりました。特に尼門跡寺院が重要と考えますのは、現在でも尚以前のように実際にお使いであるという点です。何世紀にも渡り尼門跡が創建されて以来、崇高な信仰の場でした。このように建造物が長く、意義深い歴史を秘めており、当初からまもりつがれていることは、特に大変重要なことだと考えます。その建物という形だけでなく、中にある精神もまもっていくことが大事だと思います。そういう観点から、ワールド・モニュメント財団は、チベットの仏教寺院、ローマの修道院、中国のラマ教寺院でも修復事業をおこなっております。

　ワールド・モニュメント財団が修復プロジェクトに関わることになった、300年の歴史を持つ中宮寺門跡の表御殿は、長年の使用により劣化がすすみ、また、1995年の阪神大震災により甚大な被害を受けました。ワールド・モニュメント財団は建物が安全に使用されることと、建造物の修復が充分されること、そしてそれを実現するための助成をさせていただくことにしました。目的達成には、パートナーが互いに熱心に取り組まなければ実現しないと思いますが、中宮寺、日野西光尊御門跡のお人柄と、御人徳により、ワールド・モニュメント財団と中世日本研究所から世界的な支援を得られ、結果多くの日本国内の方々からの支援も得られました。このように中宮寺門跡の修復プロジェクトは、1400年の歴史をより強固なものにするお手伝いをすることができたと自負しております。私どもは、この中宮寺門跡のプロジェクトが今後も日本の方々が民間レベルで協力され、日本の歴史的遺産である尼門跡を一緒にお見守りする先駆けとなれればと願っております。

Japanese Imperial Buddhist Convents Projects

Henry Tzu Ng, Executive Vice President, World Monuments Fund

World Monuments Fund (WMF) has worked for over forty years, in over ninety countries. The restoration of Chūgūji Imperial Convent in Nara was the most complicated and largest project undertaken by WMF in Japan. This essay describes WMF's approach to the project and how the restoration of Chūgūji Imperial Convent fits into WMF's global program of activities.

WMF is the world's most prominent private international historic preservation organization and has worked to save more than five hundred historic sites around the world. Some of these sites are well known, such as Angkor Wat in Cambodia and Marie Antoinette's theater in Versailles; others are important, but less known. WMF works in countries with varied political, social, and economic circumstances. Some are rich countries and others have fewer resources. We work in Africa, but we also work in the United States and England. We have learned that no country, no matter how rich it is, can take care of all its heritage and that there is always a role for private citizens and organizations. In every country, historic preservation needs all the help it can get.

WMF provides assistance in three ways. We often provide financial assistance, or challenge grants, to help develop stronger sources of local support, and Chūgūji brought in hundreds of new supporters when it successfully raised local funds to match a WMF/ Robert Wilson Challenge grant.

We also provide technical assistance by helping to identify key structural or design challenges, and by developing and encouraging projects that can serve as model projects for buildings facing similar problems. The Chūgūji restoration program incorporated the latest research in seismic and building safety, developed a solution to make the roof lighter in weight, and installed new fire detection and suppression systems. The efficient coordination of the exterior work with the conservation of the fine interiors will also serve as a model for other sites undergoing large scale restoration.

WMF also assists projects through advocacy by bringing attention and resources, both international and local, to help save historical sites. When WMF, as an independent international preservation organization, becomes involved with a project, such as Chūgūji, WMF can bring local attention to an historic site that merits conservation and advocacy efforts. It helps local citizens realize that they have something in their community that is valued on an international level. The conservation of the imperial Buddhist convents falls into a special category of WMF's work. WMF has helped to conserve many types of buildings around the world, but the convents are special because they are still being used today for their original purpose. For centuries since they were established the convents have been a place of continuous spiritual devotion. When a building has such a long and meaningful history and remains a living legacy to its original purpose, it is a particularly precious cultural landmark. It is very important to maintain the physical—and spiritual—continuity of such a building, and WMF is currently working on similar sites, including a Buddhist monastery in Tibet, a Christian convent in Rome, and a Buddhist lama community in China.

WMF became involved with Chūgūji because its Royal Reception Suite (Omote Goten) had sustained three hundred years of continuous use and was on the verge of succumbing to age and the elements, exacerbated by the aftershocks of the Kobe Earthquake in 1995. WMF's goal was to work with the convent to stabilize and restore the building, and help the convent improve its long-term stewardship of the site, both architecturally and financially. Goals like these cannot be achieved without enthusiastic partners. Under the spiritual and institutional leadership of Abbess Hinonishi Kōson, international support from WMF and the Institute for Medieval Japanese Studies was joined by hundreds of local supporters. In this way, the restoration of Chūgūji Imperial Convent also helped to create a stronger community to sustain Chūgūji as it enters the 1400th year of its existence. We sincerely hope that this will be a model encouraging more private citizens and groups in Japan to join hands with us to care for Japan's historic imperial convents.

中宮寺表御殿の修復

建造物の修復

はじめに

　表御殿は、中宮寺門跡の主要な建物でありながら建てられた時期は知られておらず、建築様式から判断して寺が現位置に移転した江戸時代初期、16世紀中頃から17世紀前半の創建であると考えられてきた。他の建物同様、表御殿は長年使われる間に必要に応じて手を加えられ、姿を変えてきた。修理前に本瓦葺だった屋根は、かつては檜の皮を重ねて葺く檜皮葺であり、またご本尊に備える水を組む井戸が納められている建物南西隅の杮葺の閼伽井屋は、19世紀前期に増築されたと伝わる。

　年代が確認できる最も早い時期の改修は、南面と西面の軒の出が深くされた文政5年(1822)に行われた。次いで大正7年(1918)には、檜皮葺の屋根が本瓦葺に葺き替えられた。これは、建物の耐火性を高めるためであったと思われる。同時に、今までより重厚になった屋根を受けるために軒及び小屋組は補強され、軒の出が縮められた。

表御殿外観　修復前
Suite before restoration

Restoration of the Chūgūji Royal Reception Suite

Architectural Restoration
Introduction

Due to lack of archival documents, the exact year of construction of Chūgūji Imperial Convent's Royal Reception Suite was not known. However, judging from its architectural style and characteristic features, the structure has long been considered to have been built in the early Edo period, sometime between the mid-16th and the early 17th century, when the convent relocated to its present site.

As with most ancient structures, over the convent's long history, the Suite experienced repairs and alterations, some of which drastically changed its appearance. The roof had originally been constructed of layers of Japanese cypress bark, a traditional roofing material mainly used in temple and shrine edifices. At the southwest corner, the Akaiya, a small shingle-roofed structure housing a well, from which water had been drawn for offering to the convent's revered images, was added on sometime in the first half of the 19th century.

The earliest known restoration date of the Royal Reception Suite is 1822, when the eaves that overhang the south and west facades were deepened by attaching an additional outer set of rafters.

Then, in 1918, the roofing material was changed from the original considerably lightweight bark to much heavier clay roof tiles, possibly for fireproofing. Already at that time, the carpenters realized that the deep

表御殿室内
Interior of the Suite, view to the Upper Level Chamber

北廊下、東を見る
North aisle, looking east

縁へと続く廊下を周囲に巡らされた各室は、大部分が建具で間仕切られ、建物自体を支える壁面がとても少ない開放的な形式となっている。このため本瓦葺の屋根が建物を圧迫し、重みに耐えかねた軒は下がり、建物の美しさのひとつである軒先の優雅な曲線も歪んできていた。柱の一部は湾曲し、建具の開け閉めも困難になっていた。

　1995年に発生した阪神淡路大震災は、関西地方の無数の文化財建造物に被害をもたらした。表御殿は創建以来丁寧に手入れされてきたが、最後の修復から年月を重ねており、この地震によりさらに壁にはひび割れが生じ、木部の接合部は弛み、雨漏りした箇所は腐朽し虫害も見られ、ますます早急な対応が望まれる状況になっていた。

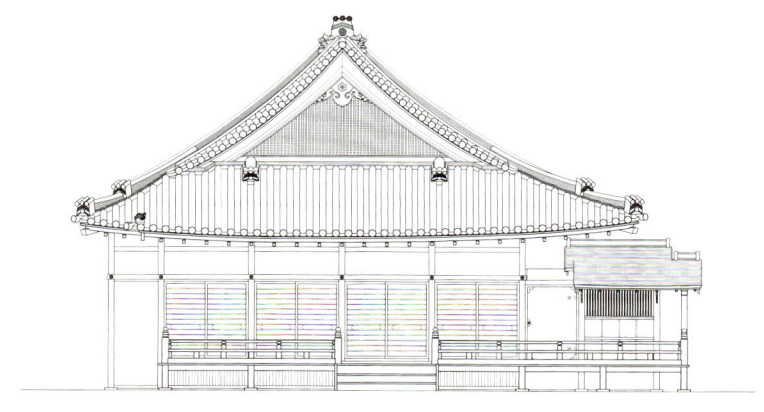

表御殿　西立面図
West side

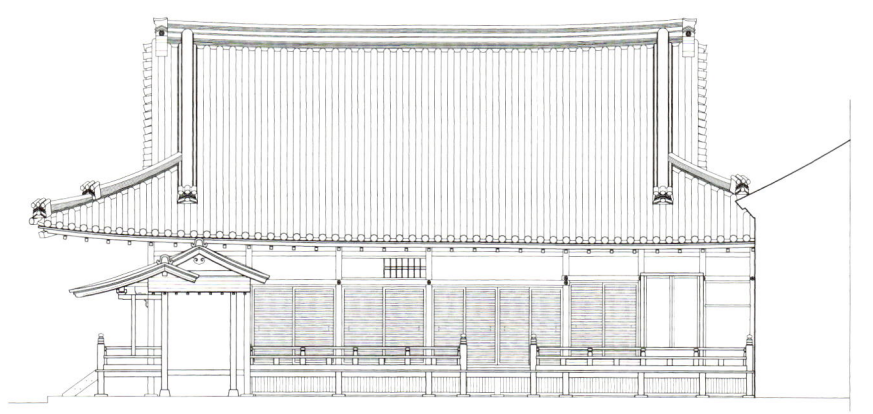

表御殿　南立面図
South side

eaves would not be able to support the heavier roof, so the eaves were again altered to make the new outer rafters shorter, and reinforcements were introduced into the roof structure, as well as to the eaves. However, this was still not adequate, and as a result contributed to the damage leading to the 2008 restoration.

In this structure, there were not enough earthen partition walls to act as structural supports. The smooth flowing curves of the eaves, one of the beautiful architectural features of this famous convent, had been warped by the weight of the roof. Several of the comparatively thin columns had curved or tilted under the roof pressure, and the sliding screens could no longer be shut tight. Where rainwater entered the structure, parts of the building had become prone to insect damage and wood rot.

The devastating Kobe Earthquake of 1995, which destroyed and damaged countless historic structures in the Kansai area, hit Nara as well and damaged the Royal Reception Suite. Though the structure had been well maintained, decades had passed since the last restoration, and this natural disaster became a trigger for further damage, creating cracks in walls and loosening joints between wooden structural parts.

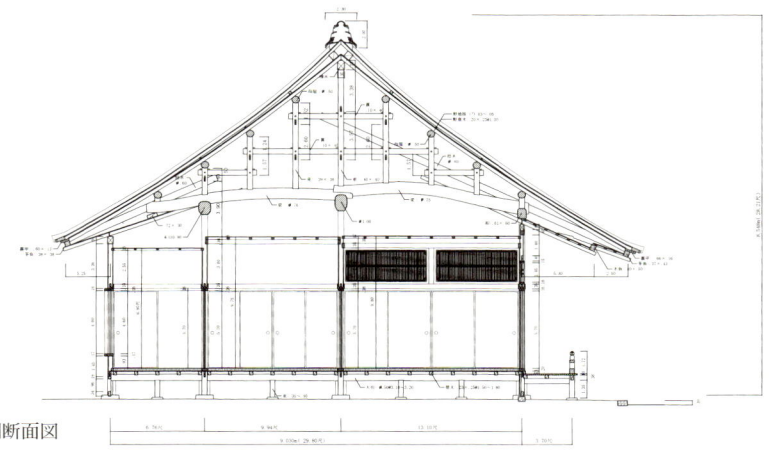

表御殿　梁間断面図
Section

修復の概要

　今回の修復の目指すところは、今後少なくとも100年は大きな修繕をしなくて済むようにすることであり、また建物を日常的に利用するうえで使いやすくかつ安全にすることであった。大震災の被害を受け、建物の弱点は既にあらわになっていたが、まず修復に先立ち建物全体の構造診断が実施された。その結果、壁が少ないこの建物に対して本瓦葺の屋根が重すぎ、躯体の補強が必要であることが指摘された。

　屋根荷重を軽減するために大正修復以前の檜皮葺に戻すことも検討されたが、本瓦葺に変更されてから月日を重ねた現状の姿は、広く親しまれている。隣に立つ本堂は既に本瓦葺になっていた表御殿と調和する意匠で設計されている。しかし、依然として表御殿の屋根を軽くしなければならない。

　従ってこの修復では、屋根の葺き替えが最大の課題となった。構造補強に加え、傷みが生じていた木部や土壁、畳、錺金物にも手が入れられた。修復は、現代の建築工法では失われつつある日本の伝統技術を受け継ぐ、各分野の第一人者たちの技を結集して行われた。さらには建物を火災からまもるための防災設備も新たにされた。建物の修復と同時に行われた襖や壁を飾る障壁画の修復については、別項で取り上げる。

修復前の屋根　軒先の瓦が垂下していた
Sagging roof tiles at the eaves before restoration

土壁には割れが生じていた
Cracks on the earthen walls

南面の柱は、屋根の荷重を受けて湾曲していた
Columns of the south facade buckled under the weight of the roof

Outline of Restoration

The main aim of the 2008 restoration project was to make the structure sturdy and safe in order to withstand the next hundred years without another major restoration. It was executed with the help of the highest level master craftsmen from all areas of specialization, such as carpentry, roof tile production and roof construction, earthen wall plastering, architectural metalworking, tatami mat making, and restoration of paintings on paper. Such traditional Japanese building crafts are quickly disappearing from the contemporary construction scene, and the best specialists had to be sought.

Because the 1995 earthquake had made apparent the structure's weakness, a thorough structural survey was executed in the process of designing this restoration. As expected, the result of this analysis made clear that the weight of the clay tile roof was excessive for the fragile wood frame of the Suite's building, which was not designed to support such a roof to begin with. If the 20th century tiled roof were to be kept, installation of reinforcements between the columns could not be avoided. How could a structure, where the sliding screens of every room can be opened up to create a single connected space, be reinforced with columns without obstructing the view? This was a major dilemma.

It had been close to a century since the roofing had been changed to clay roof tiles, and people today were used to seeing that roof. The new main worship hall, a separate building, had been designed in the 1960s, taking into consideration the architectural style of the Royal Reception Suite as it was then. Thus, the current abbess Hinonishi Kōson strongly insisted on maintaining the present outward appearance of the Suite.

Reroofing became the focal point of the restoration, in addition to structural reinforcement, repairs of wooden architectural parts, earthen walls, tatami mats, metal fixtures, and the installation of a fire prevention system. The polychrome paintings on walls and fusuma sliding screens, which will be dealt with separately in the following section, were carefully removed and restored by specialists.

修復の開始

　2007年夏、いよいよ念願であった表御殿の修復が開始された。まず、工事の安全を願って厳かに起工式が行われた。前年に国の登録有形文化財となった建物に対して行われる修復では、文化財修復・建築歴史・建築構造・行政などの各分野の専門家たちを含む委員会が設置され、修復を通して表御殿の価値が確実に将来に受け継がれるよう、指導がなされた。

　はじめに修復中の建物を風雨からまもる覆いが設けられた。屋根も葺き替えるので、素屋根と呼ばれる屋根が架けられた。奈良県下の文化財修復現場では、近年見ることが稀になった、丸太を番線で組み上げる昔ながらの技法を今日も継承している。中宮寺は、風致地区にも指定されている国史跡中宮寺跡内に位置するので、この仮設物が景観に及ぼす影響に配慮し、足場周囲のシートは落ち着いた灰色にされた。

　修復前の屋根では瓦の並びに乱れが生じ、瓦自体にも傷みが見られた。瓦は一枚一枚丁寧に降ろされた。屋根を下地から補修し、使える瓦は再利用しながら全面的に葺き替える計画であった。

起工式　2007年8月
Groundbreaking ceremony in August 2007

丸太で組んだ足場と素屋根
Roofed scaffolding assembled using logs and wire

屋根から平瓦を降ろす
Dismantling concave roof tiles

杉皮の屋根下地
Japanese cedar bark waterproofing layer

Restoration Begins

The long-awaited restoration of the Royal Reception Suite was finally begun in the summer of 2007. A groundbreaking ceremony was held to pray for safety throughout the course of the project.

Restoration of this Nationally Registered Cultural Property, so designated in 2006, was executed under the supervision of an architectural conservator in tandem with a preservation commission created specifically for this project, in order to make sure that the true significance of this landmark would be maintained and enhanced through the process. Members of the committee included specialists from such fields as architectural restoration, architectural history, and structural design, as well as an official from the Nara city government.

First, a roofed scaffolding was constructed to cover the entire building so that the Suite, especially when its roofing had been dismantled, would be protected from wind and rain, and also so that the restoration schedule would not be influenced by bad weather, particularly during the long rainy season in early summer. Nara is one of the few prefectures in Japan preserving a traditional Japanese technique of scaffolding by binding logs with wire at restoration sites, instead of using conventional modern metal scaffolding systems. All through the project, the outside of the scaffolding was covered with gray-colored netting, instead of the commonly used bright blue-colored tarp-like covering, so as not to add a discordant note to the view of the historic landscape of the temple grounds, which is designated a National Historic Site, as well as a Prefectural Scenic District.

Over the ages, the smooth alignment of the roof tiles had become disrupted, and loose tiles at the eave ends had sagged. Many tiles had weathered severely or had cracked and needed to be checked individually to see if they could be reused, and so the roof tiles were carefully removed from the roof one by one.

重たい屋根の問題

　瓦は本瓦葺と呼ばれる、平瓦と丸瓦とを組み合わせて葺く形式である。大正年間までの屋根は、本瓦葺より軽い檜皮葺であった。前述のように屋根葺き替え時に木部は補強されていたが十分ではなく、このままでは大きな地震が来たら間違いなく被害を被ることになる。

　文化財の修復では、建物を健全にすることが第一であるが、同時に建物の歴史上価値が最も高いと考えられる過去の姿に復原することも、広く行われている。中宮寺表御殿を創建当初の姿に戻すのであれば、深くされた軒の出を文政修復前のかたちに戻し、屋根を再び檜皮で葺くことも考えられた。こうすれば、確かに建物にかかる荷重を減らすことはできるが、費用が高額であるうえに今後30年から40年周期で葺き替えが必要となるため、この案は見送られた。

　そこで編み出されたのが、瓦の代わりに銅板を本瓦葺の平瓦と丸瓦のかたちに加工して葺く方法である。そうすれば屋根の見かけを大きく変えることなく重量を今までの1/10まで軽くできるうえ、落ち着いた雰囲気を醸し出す深い軒を保つこともできる。

本瓦葺き　丸瓦と平瓦を組み合わせて葺く
Detail of the clay tile roof employing convex and concave tiles

修復前の本瓦葺の屋根遠景
Clay tile roof before restoration

修復前の軒瓦
Clay eave end tiles, before restoration

Problematic Roof

Here the trouble begins. The roof before restoration was in a style employing two types of tiles, vault-shaped convex tiles and slightly curved concave tiles. First, the concave tiles had been laid out on the sheathing boards over Japanese cedar bark, which acted as a waterproof layer, and mud was used to hold the tiles in place. Then the convex tiles had been placed so as to cover the vertical joints between the concave tiles. This was obviously too much of a burden for the delicately built Suite structure. If the building were struck by another large earthquake, further damage would be inevitable.

In the restoration of cultural properties, though repairing damage remains the main goal, structures are often restored back to their appearance in a historical period deemed most significant in their architectural heritage, so that it presents the most appropriate historic face to be handed down to the next generations. In the case of this Suite, to bring the structure back to its original composition when first erected, the eaves would have had to be shortened considerably and the roof covered with Japanese cypress bark. Such an alteration, however, would require very costly periodical reroofing every thirty to forty years, and would become an additional financial burden on Chūgūji convent. Nevertheless, given the realities of the needed repair, either this elegant and airy structure would have to be newly and heavily reinforced or the roof would have to be made lighter for the Royal Reception Suite to survive in the centuries to come.

After reviewing various possibilities, an alternative plan was devised that would maintain the present appearance and at the same time decrease the weight of the roof. The innovative idea was to use copper sheets to create a tile-shaped roofing material over a wood frame, so as to simulate the desired appearance. The weight of this roofing method amounts to barely one-tenth of that of clay roof tiles. Thereby, the deep eave overhangs could be retained.

表御殿の建築年代が判明した大棟での発見

　ここで今回の修復の大きな発見があった。江戸時代の職人がこの瓦を造る時に、大棟の東端に据えられていた獅子口の上面に箆で文字を削り込んでいたのだ。ここには「石見椽橘吉長／法隆寺瓦師／与源左衛門／同権四郎／元禄九丙子／十一月／大阪茂右衛門」とあり、元禄9年（1696）の瓦の製作年代が判明した。このような部材に記された年代は、建物が建てられた時に近いと判断され、他にこの時期を決定づける棟札のようなものがない場合には、建築年代の根拠とされる。この獅子口は部分的に欠けていたため屋根の上に戻さず、建物の歴史を伝える重要な部材として、保存されることとなった。

　中宮寺というたいへん由緒ある門跡でありながら、表御殿の建築年代を示す史料は今までみつかっておらず、この獅子口の発見によりこの時期が初めて明らかになった。

　かつての本堂であった観音堂は、元禄3年（1690）に建てられたことが知られており、今回中宮寺の重要な建物である本堂と表御殿が、ほぼ同時期に新築されていたこともわかった。この観音堂は昭和43年（1968）の現本堂の新築に先立ち、高野山の五坊寂静院に移築されている。

旧本堂（観音堂）外観
Former main worship hall (Kannondō)

旧本堂（観音堂）堂内
Former main worship hall (Kannondō) interior

Discovery Revealing the Period of the Suite's Construction

Here, we must not forget to mention the exciting discovery made during the course of dismantling the roof tiles. On the topside of the decorative lion-mouthed ridge tile attached to the end of the main ridge was found an inscription, including the date of 1696, written with a palette knife by the original tile craftsman.

Generally, the year inscribed on a ridge tag marks the time of construction or restoration, but one for this historic structure had never been found. The exact year the roof tiles were made now became clear, which is probably not too far from the year of completion of the entire structure. Discovering definitive historical evidence like this adds additional luster to the accomplishments of this restoration.

Because the lion-mouthed ridge tile with the inscription had cracks and missing parts, and could no longer be used on the roof, it will be preserved and displayed as an historical artifact.

Though Chūgūji is an Imperial Convent with a highly distinguished history, no documents recording the year of construction of the Royal Reception Suite have been uncovered to this day. The former main worship hall (Kannondō), which once stood next to the Suite, is known to have been erected in the third year of Genroku (1690). This hall was transferred to Gobōjakujōin, a Buddhist temple on Mount Kōya, prior to the construction of the present main worship hall in 1968. Thus, it became apparent for the first time that Chūgūji's two major structures, the main worship hall and the Royal Reception Suite, had been constructed in the early Genroku era (1688-1703), making these years a key period of construction in the long history of this originally 7th-century temple.

大棟獅子口正面
Lion-mouthed roof tile

大棟獅子口上端の箆書き
「石見橡橘吉長／法隆寺瓦師／与源左衛門／同権四郎／元禄九丙子／十一月／大阪茂右衛門」
Inscription of the year 1696 on the lion-mouthed roof tile

銅板で葺かれた新しい屋根

　屋根を軽くすることだけが目的であれば、本堂と同様の平らな銅板葺にすることも考えられたが、御前様のご意向を受け、修復前と雰囲気が変わらない、屋根面に陰影をつくる本瓦型の銅板葺にされた。

　今まで葺かれていた軒先の本瓦には、丸瓦に菊花紋、平瓦に大正修復時の年号を示す「大正中宮寺戊午」の文字が入れられていた。新しい銅板瓦ではこの意匠に倣い、丸瓦は同じ模様で造り、平瓦には修復完成年である平成20年の干支を、御前様のお書きになった文字で「平成中宮寺戊子」と型押しした。各瓦の寸法は今までと同じであるので、屋根の材質は異なるが輪郭は変わっていない。

　銅板で屋根を葺くために、まず木材による下地を造った。この上に、銅板瓦をひとつひとつ互いに端を折り込み繋げながら、屋根面全体を葺き上げた。

　屋根頂上の大棟や隅棟などは、修復前と同様の瓦積みにした。各棟先端の鬼瓦や獅子口を銅線で木部に止め付け、漆喰を用いて棟を積み上げた。いったん降ろした瓦は丁寧に調査し、再度使えるものと使えないものとに選別した。傷んでいてもはや使えなくなった瓦を補う分は、今までの瓦と同じ形式で新たに製作した。

　葺き上がったばかりの屋根は鮮やかに輝いていたが、時間が経つにつれて焦げ茶色に変色し周囲の景観に馴染み、遠目に見ると一見本瓦葺と見まがうほどである。なお建物は風致地区内に位置するので、今回の外観の変更にあたっては、手続きのうえ実施する必要があった。

銅板葺軒詳細
Copper roof, eave end detail

軒丸瓦頭
Convex 'tile'

軒平瓦頭
Concave 'tile'

銅板で製作した本瓦型瓦
Copper roofing 'tiles' for eave ends in the shape of clay roof tiles

New Copper Roofing

A flat copper roofing style, similar to that of the present main worship hall, could have been adopted to decrease the load of the roof. However, the Abbess preferred a roof with the same irregular surface that yields 'shadow and light' in order to maintain the look of the familiar clay roof tiles of the past hundred years of the convent.

The visible edges of clay roof tiles along the eave ends are decorated with distinctive motifs. At Chūgūji, the design of a chrysanthemum blossom with sixteen petals derived from the imperial crest was employed on the convex tiles and Chinese characters indicating the reroofing year (1918) adorned the concave tiles. The designs of the new copper eave end 'tiles' reflect these clay-tile patterns. Concave copper tile-ends were pressed with chrysanthemums, while the convex ones were pressed with Chinese characters in the same style, but with the year 2008 in the Abbess's handwriting. The measurements of these 'tiles' were made the same as those of clay, so that the silhouette of the roof would be retained.

Roofing with cooper, however, involves a process that is different from clay tiles. First, a wooden framework was constructed on the sheathing boards, and then copper 'tiles' were placed on it, joining the seams of each 'tile' together to create a large membrane covering the entire roof.

On the other hand, the ridges on the top and corners of the roof were kept in the same style as before, using only clay tiles, layering the convex roof tiles face down with mud and plaster. Every single clay tile of these ridges had been inspected after being dismantled in order to determine whether or not it could be reused. To replace damaged or missing tiles, large sculptural tiles were newly made to decorate the ridge-ends.

The sight of the brightly shining new pink roof first came as a shock to those who saw it, but as months passed, the copper surface eventually gained a brown patina and is expected to turn into a favorable deep green shade in several years, when it will blend naturally into its surroundings. Because the Royal Reception Suite stands within a designated Scenic District of Nara Prefecture, official permission from the Prefectural government had to be obtained for this change in appearance.

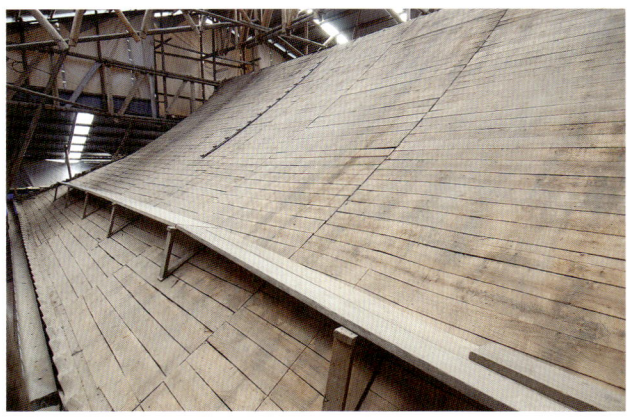

中宮寺表御殿の修復
RESTORATION OF THE CHŪGŪJI ROYAL RECEPTION SUITE

杉皮解体後の屋根
Roof after cedar bark layer was taken down

修復前の瓦の葺き土の厚さを補うために、新たに捨垂木と野地を組み立てる
New set of rafters and sheathing boards replacing layer of earth used for roofing

捨垂木の上に野地板を張る
Sheathing boards placed on new rafters

屋根下地完了
Foundations for copper roofing

本瓦型銅板瓦で屋根を葺く
Reroofing with copper sheets, replicating outline of former clay tile roof

完成した本瓦型銅板葺
New copper roof

中宮寺表御殿の修復
RESTORATION OF THE CHŪGŪJI ROYAL RECEPTION SUITE

木部の補修

　木部に大きな破損はなかったが、地震により各部材の柱との取り付け部が緩んだり、隙間が開いたりしている箇所については、それぞれ丁寧に補修した。修復する範囲の木部をいったん取り外す際には、各部材を前の場所に戻せるよう、番付を書いた板を止めつけた。補修に用いる木材は、もとの部材に使われている木材と同じ材種や材質はもちろんのこと、木目の具合も揃えたものを選んだ。場所ごとの傷み具合を正確に判断し、手を入れる範囲は最小限に抑えて繕った。

　修復を通して木製の部材を取り替えたり補修したりすると、同じ材種の木材であっても300年以上風化した部材と比べると、色合いが異なる。そこで、小さい範囲の補修では、もはや使えなくなった部材の端材を用いて補修する。あるいは新たな木材を用いる場合には、古色塗を施し、周囲と調和させる。新しく取り替えた部材には、後年になっても修復の範囲がわかるように、見えないところに修復年の入った焼き印を押したり、年号を記したりしている。

　建具の建て付けが狂ったり、框や桟が欠けていれば、破損箇所のみを補修した。また失われていた建具は、既存のものと同じように複製して補った。特に重い板戸や舞良戸が取り付く箇所では、敷居が甚だしく擦り減っていた

修復前の懸魚(げぎょ)は著しく風化していた
Severely weathered west gable pendant

修復後の懸魚　もとの彫刻と同じ様につくり直した
Damaged gable pendant replaced by replicating the original

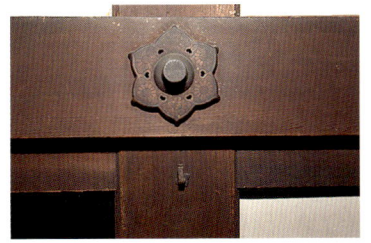

古い長押釘隠し金物
Old metalwork on a non-penetrating beam

欠損していた金物は既存品に倣って製作した
Missing metalwork replicated based on old samples

Restoration of Wooden Parts

Though there was no serious structural damage to the wooden parts of the building, some beams had weathered or worn out, and many joints had become loose after the earthquake or over centuries of continued use, all of which needed to be carefully repaired. New wood of the same species and grade was selected for repairs, and, where necessary, wood grains were matched. The extent of the damage, as well as its causes, was surveyed and treated accordingly, keeping repairs and replacement parts to a minimum. All the building parts temporarily dismantled for repairs were systematically numbered, in order to make sure that they would be placed back in their respective original positions.

In the case of the sliding screens, if rails, stiles, or door panels had loosened, been chipped, or had rotted, only the damaged areas were patched or replaced. Missing door fixtures were replicated according to extant samples, using the same traditional carpentry techniques.

Because there were very few walls in this Suite that could be used for introducing reinforcement, the extant wooden sliding panels with decorative horizontal crosspieces (mairado), located along the aisles on the outer perimeter of the building, were employed for strengthening the structure. These doors were papered on the interior and therefore could hide reinforcement placed under their surfaces, if such reinforcements could be made flat and thin. Thus, carbon fiber strips were adhered onto these doors on the inner side, and the inner surface was covered with eggshell-colored Japanese paper, as had originally been the case.

Particularly where there are heavy wooden board doors and mairado, the sills had become worn out and the corners of these channels had been rounded. Here, either the entire channel was removed and replaced with new material, or just the bottom of the channels was dug out and filled with bamboo strips, so that the doors would slide smoothly again.

In 1971, the interior of the Upper Level Chamber, the highest level room in the Suite, where the princess-abbess would sit in audience, had been cleansed with caustic soda and refinished with wax, which at the time was considered effective for beautifying the room, but which over

ので、敷居の溝の中を彫り込み、竹材を敷き、滑らかに開け閉めできるようにした。

　壁面が非常に少ない建物自体をどのように強固にするかが一番の問題であったが、廊下と屋外を仕切る舞良戸を補強する案が採用された。これらの戸の室内側は、もともと紙張りで仕上げられていたので、この下に薄く平らな帯状の炭素繊維を張ることで、視覚的に室内を損なうことなく、壁面を強くすることができた。

　最も大切な空間である御上段の間においては、昭和46年（1971）にくすんでいた内装の見栄えを良くするために、柱や長押などの白木だった木肌は苛性ソーダで洗浄のうえワックス仕上げされていた。この改修から時間が経ち表面はまだらになり、決して美しいとは言えない状態になっていた。この部屋では木部を傷めることがないように留意しながらワックス塗を除去し、往時の荘厳を取り戻した。

表御殿の安全のために

　表御殿は、渡り廊下によって北側では大玄関を経て客殿と、南側では本堂と繋がり、建物間には仕切りがない。日常的に利用される生活空間でもある客殿や庫裏と、ハレの場である表御殿とを、防災計画上何らかのかたちで分離する必要があった。そこで表御殿への入口となる渡り廊下には、現代的な防火戸が新設された。自動火災報知設備としては、室内の目障りとならないよう従来型の煙感知器や熱感知器は使わず、空気管と呼ばれる被覆銅線を各室天井周囲に張り巡らせることで対処した。

　このように表御殿の建物の修復は、隅々まで細心の注意を払いながら進められたのである。

表御殿の周囲を囲む舞良戸
Mairado screen doors on the outer perimeters of the Suite

舞良戸は帯状の炭素繊維を張り、補強する
舞良戸は修復前と同様に紙張りにするので、補強は隠れる
Reinforcement of mairado screen doors using carbon fiber strips hidden under a covering of Japanese paper

the years had resulted in a patchy discoloration of the wood surfaces. This finish was removed with great care, so as not to damage the wood itself, and the grandeur of this special room was thereby revived.

There is always the issue of patina. When new wood material is introduced in restoration, whether it is of the same species, grade, or grain, its appearance will differ from wood that has aged over three hundred years. Should new material be finished to make it appear old, so as to match the extant material? If the area to be repaired is small, weathered material discarded from a damaged area elsewhere in the building can be used. Generally, in the case of a larger repair or complete replacement by professional Japanese architectural restoration conservators, patina is applied either with a colorant that doubles as a wood preservative, or by a matching pigment created through blending traditional materials, such as red earth pigment, ochre, persimmon tannin, and pine soot. To distinguish the new 'old-looking' parts, the year of restoration is branded or written onto hidden surfaces, so that future architects and carpenters will not be deceived by the perfection of modern craftsmanship.

Safety of the Suite

By way of open hallways, the Royal Reception Suite is connected with the guest hall of the convent, via the Grand Entrance to the north, and with the main worship hall to the south. Therefore, as fire preventive measures, it was necessary to create some kind of partition between the Suite, which is used only on special occasions, and the other structures used on a daily basis. Modern fireproof doors were newly installed where the Suite meets the connecting hallways.

Conventional fire prevention systems involving modern equipment, such as smoke and heat detectors, would clash with the ambience of the interior, and so a heat detection system, using very thin copper tubes placed discreetly around the ceiling corners of each room, was installed.

障壁画の修復
表御殿の室内

　木造平屋建て入母屋造の表御殿は、正面を西に向けて立つ。周囲に縁が巡らされた建物に入ると、南北2列に6部屋が並び、西及び北側には幅広い畳敷きの廊下が回る。建物の南列には奥から御上段の間、一の間、二の間、北列には吉野竜田の間、御三帖、猿の間と続く。

　各室は障壁画の張られた壁や襖によって間仕切られ、廊下側の障子から柔らかい日差しが差し込む。この平面計画は、桃山時代までに確立された書院造の形式を踏襲している。

　最も奥に位置する上段の間には、大床と棚、付書院が備えられ、他の部屋より床が一段高くなっている。さらには、他の部屋の天井は簡素な竿縁天井であるのに対して、ここでは格天井にされていることからも、この部屋が建物の中でも一番重要な空間であることが読み取れる。

　表御殿は、今日に至るまで非常に限られた方々によってのみ使用されてきた。今でも宮家の方々がお見えの時は、この表御殿で迎えられる。謁見の間となる上段の間の手前2部屋は控えの間となり、特に一の間は上級の尼僧たちが謁見の進行を司るために座した場所である。上段の間北隣りの吉野竜田の間は、かつて門跡の住まいとして利用されたこともあったようである。前の御三帖と猿の間は、この控えの間となる。現在門跡での茶会開催時には吉野竜田の間を待ち合いに、他の部屋を水屋などとして用いている。

　壁や襖の紙張りには、部屋によって主題の異なる手彩色の障壁画が描かれている。これらの障壁画は、美術工芸品や古文書の修復において経験を積んだ京都の工房によって念入りに修復された。

御上段の間　大床と付書院
Upper Level Chamber, alcove and built-in desk

Restoration of Wall Paintings
Rooms of the Royal Reception Suite

The floor plan of the Suite consists of two rows of three aligned rooms, totaling six continuous straw-matted chambers in all. It is surrounded by wide matted aisles on the west and north sides, with an exterior veranda along the west and south walls. This is a classic composition for aristocratic residential structures of the shoin-style, established in the Momoyama period (1573-1614). The south row consists of the Upper Level Chamber (Jōdan no ma), the First Room (Ichi no ma), and the Second Room (Ni no ma), and the north row includes the Throne Room (Yoshino Tatsuta no ma), a small Three Matted Room (Gosanjō), and the Monkey Room (Saru no ma).

The use of the Royal Reception Suite has been limited to very few members of the convent and is employed today in welcoming guests from the imperial family. The two rooms leading to the Upper Level Chamber were used as antechambers for those to be received in audience by the princess-abbess. Particularly, the First Room was where nuns of higher-class assisting the proceedings of the audience were seated. The Throne Room was formerly the living quarters for princess-abbesses, and the two preceding rooms (the Three Matted Room and the Monkey Room) functioned as its antechambers. Today, when tea ceremonies are performed at the convent, the Throne Room is used as a waiting room for guests, while preparations are made in the other two rooms.

There are decorative paintings of varying themes on the paper-faced fusuma doors and partition walls, making each space distinct. Translucent paper-covered shoji screens along the wide aisles encircling these interior spaces allow natural light into the dim interior.

The Upper Level Chamber, the innermost and most prestigious room, has a wide decorative alcove and a shelf in the side alcove, with a built-in desk arrangement on the side wall. The walls and fusuma doors are entirely covered with paintings of flowers and birds on a brilliant gold background, creating a heavenly atmosphere. The floor is elevated a step higher than the rest of the rooms, which also signifies the superior status

修復前の障壁画には染みが生じ、紙が破れている箇所も見られた。また、彩色が色褪せたり、部分的に彩色が剥落したりしているところもあった。建物から取り外された障壁画の修復は、それぞれ傷みの状況と度合いに応じて、以下の処置を組み合わせた7段階に分類して行われた。

　絵画本紙の裏には、肌裏紙が直接張られ、その上に裏打ち紙が数枚張られている。絵画の傷み具合に応じて、修復の際にこれらの裏打ち紙をどこまで剥がすかが決められ、絵画自体の修復方法も決定される。傷みが最も進んでいた絵画については、絵画の描かれている本紙の裏打ち紙を剥がしたうえで、汚れを落とし、肌裏紙を張り直す大規模な修復が行われた。

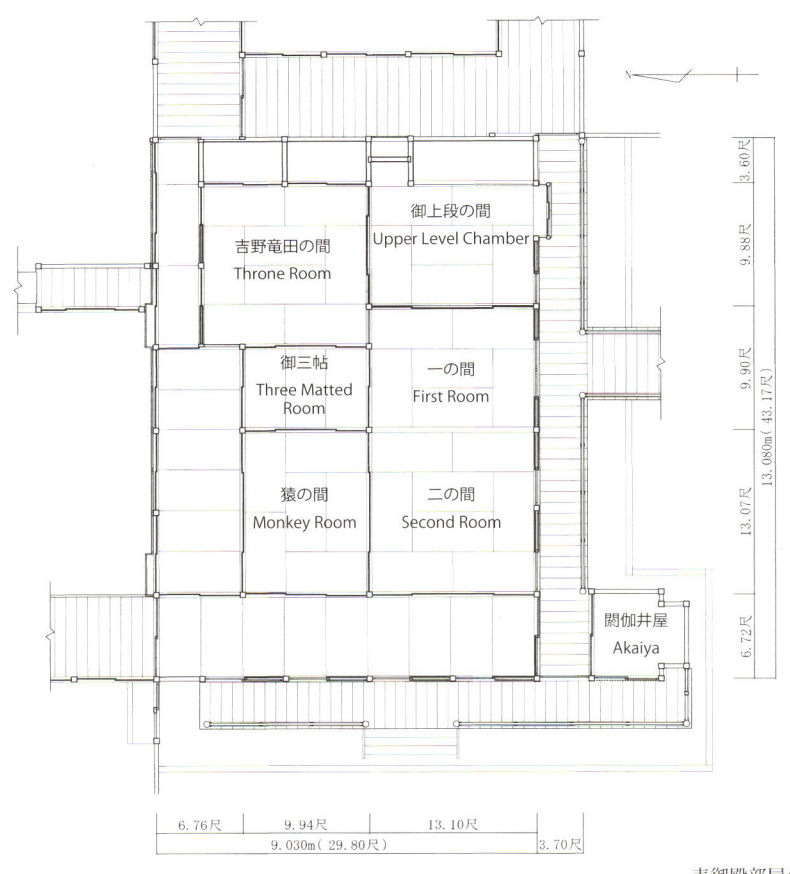

表御殿部屋名称図
Floor plan of the Suite

御上段の間　瑞鳥瑞花図
Upper Level Chamber　Paintings of flowers and phoenix birds

一の間　唐子遊戯図
First Room　Paintings of Chinese children at play

二の間（南面）　唐子遊戯図
Second Room (south wall)　Paintings of Chinese children at play

二の間（北面）　唐子遊戯図
Second Room (north wall)　Paintings of Chinese children at play

吉野竜田の間（南面、東面）　吉野桜図
Throne Room (south and east walls)　Seasonal landscape paintings of cherry blossoms in Yoshino

吉野竜田の間（北面、西面）　竜田紅葉図
Throne Room (north and west walls)　Seasonal landscape paintings of colored Japanese maple trees in Tatsuta

中宮寺表御殿の修復　RESTORATION OF THE CHŪGŪJI ROYAL RECEPTION SUITE

修　復

主な工程を、御上段の間及び一の間の障壁画の大規模修復を例に見る。

1. 建物から取り外す
   修復前の状態を記録するために写真撮影を行い、障壁画を建物から取り外した。壁に張られた絵画は、取り外しの際に傷めないように丁寧に取り扱った。建具は、工房に持ち帰ってから絵画を外した。
2. 裏打紙を剥がす
   絵画裏面に直接接着された肌裏紙以外の裏打ち紙を、取り除いた。
3. 絵の具層の剥落止め
   顔料を膠に混ぜた絵の具で描かれた絵画は、経年により膠が劣化し、顔料が剥がれることがある。剥離が著しい箇所は、傷みの状態に応じて濃度を変えた膠水溶液または布海苔入り膠水溶液で押さえた。
4. 汚れを落とす
   絵画表面に埃や汚れが付着している場合には、噴霧器を用いて表面を精製水で湿らせ、下に敷いた吸い取り紙に汚れを移した。
5. 本紙の破れ及び欠損部の補修
   障壁画の背景と色合いが調和するように染めた和紙を張り、補強した。
6. 肌裏紙の交換と補彩
   絵画の裏側から浮いた肌裏紙を新しく張り直した。修復には、楮を漉いた和紙を、用途別に産地ごとの特徴を考慮して選んだ。補修紙で補填した失われた箇所には補筆して、めだたないようにした。
7. 襖及び壁への張り込み
   修復を終えた絵画は、下地に張り込んで、引き手を取り付けた。壁に取り付くものは、修復前と同様に張り込んだ。

修理前の室内
Damaged paintings before restoration

室内の障壁画をすべて取り外した
All paintings on walls and screens dismantled

of this space. The ceiling is coffered, in contrast with all the other rooms in simpler board and batten style.

On the paper covering of fusuma screens and walls are paintings depicting birds, animals, children, plants, and seasonal scenery. These paintings were meticulously restored by Kyoto craftsmen highly experienced in restoration of fine art and archival documents.

Before restoration, many of the paintings had stains or tears, and the paint layers were discolored and partially flaking. Once removed from the structure, the paintings were individually inspected to determine what restoration procedure would be most appropriate based on the degree and cause of damage.

Restoration was undertaken by a combination of various treatments. The paintings to be restored were divided into seven groups, with treatment ranging from consolidation of flaking paint layers to intensive restoration involving complete disassembly of the backing layers.

Paintings on paper are directly reinforced on the backside with a thin paper lining, and additionally backed up by a few more layers of paper. For paintings with severe damage, all the backing layers down to the thin paper lining were removed, while for those with less damage, only the additional backing layers were taken away or none were removed at all. Soiled surfaces were cleaned and tears were patched. After the paintings had been treated, all the reinforcement backing layers were reapplied.

Restoration

The outline of this major restoration will be illustrated below through examples of treatments for severely damaged paintings of the Upper Level Chamber and the First Room.

1. Dismantling paintings

> To record the condition of the paintings before restoration, they were first photographed and then removed from the walls with much care. After taking the fittings and wall paintings to an off-site atelier, the fittings were disassembled to remove the paintings for restoration.

本紙より襲木(おそいぎ)をはずす
Screen disassembled to remove the painting

解体　旧下地より本紙をはずす
Backing layers removed from the painting

本紙に剝落止めを施す
Flaking painting layers consolidated with animal glue

表面から精製水を霧吹きで吹き付ける
Purified water sprayed onto the painted surface

本紙の汚れが、下に敷いた吸い取り紙に移る
Soiling blotted off onto Japanese paper placed underneath

裏打ち紙をはがす
Paper reinforcement on the backside removed

2. Removal of backing layers

    All backing layers, except for the thin reinforcement lining, were removed.

3. Consolidation of flaking paint layers

    Paint layers originally drawn with pigments dissolved in an aqueous solution of animal glue tend to peel off over time due to the deterioration of the glue. In order to repair substantial damage, concentrations of various solutions of animal glue, in some cases combined with seaweed, were used to consolidate the flaking layers.

4. Cleaning

    Stained painted surfaces were sprayed with purified water, and the soiling was blotted off onto Japanese paper placed underneath.

5. Repair of tears and holes

    Japanese paper, colored to match the background of the painting, was applied to the tears and holes.

6. Replacement of paper reinforcement and paint touch-up

    Paper reinforcement that had peeled away from the painted paper was newly replaced using Japanese paper made from fibers of mulberry trees. Qualities unique to paper made in different regions of Japan were considered in choosing appropriate materials for restoration. Areas where the artwork had been patched were touched up to make them unnoticeable.

7. Installation of paintings on screens and walls

    After the restored paintings were placed back on the screen doors, the frame was assembled and the original hand pulls were reattached. Paintings from the partition walls were also reinstalled in the same way as before the restoration.

中宮寺表御殿の修復 / RESTORATION OF THE CHŪGŪJI ROYAL RECEPTION SUITE

裏打ちを張り直す
New reinforcement paper applied

補修紙が補塡された箇所に補彩する
Patched areas touched up

舞良戸へ本紙を張り込む
Painting pasted back onto the wood panel door

建具の襲木（おそいぎ）をもとに戻す
Rails and stiles placed back on the wood panel door

引き手を元通りに取り付ける
Door pull reattached

絵画の周囲を四分一で押さえる
Thin black lacquered wood pieces attached on inside corners around the painting

絵の具剥離　修復前
Peeling paint before restoration

修復後
After restoration

本紙欠失　修復前
Hole in painting before restoration

修復後
After restoration

中宮寺表御殿の修復
RESTORATION OF THE CHŪGŪJI ROYAL RECEPTION SUITE

なお御三帖の間と猿の間の長押上の壁に飾られていた三十六歌仙絵は優れた作品であるが後設されたものであったため、各部屋の襖の絵画とは異質であった。加えて保存状態が良くなかったので、修復後は元の位置に戻さず別途保存し、他の展示方法を考えることとした。

本紙亀裂　修復前
Tear in painting before restoration

修復後
After restoration

The Thirty-six Poets paintings (Kasen-zu), which depict images of distinguished historical poets, had decorated the upper walls of the Three Matted Room and the Monkey Room. Although they are fine works of art, because they were later additions to the interior, and also because they were very fragile even after restoration, the decision was made not to paste them back onto the walls. Instead, there are plans to display these paintings in a safer and more portable style in the convent sometime in the future.

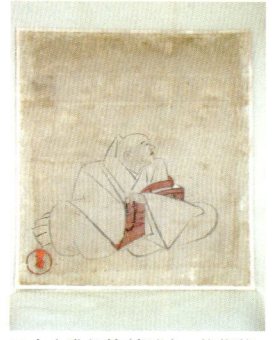

三十六歌仙絵（部分）　修復後
Three of the Thirty-six Poets, after restoration

猿の間（東面）　猿、三十六歌仙絵　修復前
Monkey Room, before restoration
(east wall) Monkeys with gold clouds
(upper wall) Thirty-six Poets

猿の間（南面）　鶴、三十六歌仙絵　修復前
Monkey Room, before restoration
(south wall) Winter landscape with cranes
(upper wall) Thirty-six Poets

おわりに

 2008年11月30日には、修復を終えたばかりの表御殿が、関係者に披露された。この後数ヶ月にわたり、今まで少数の人しか窺い知ることのできなかった表御殿の室内の様子が、初めて一般公開された。

 修復完了時には棟札を作成し、工事実施時期及び関係者の名前、工事の概要などを墨で書き、平成の修復の内容が後世に伝えられるようにした。修復の詳細を記した報告書も刊行される予定である。この修復により、建物の新しい歴史がつくられた。

 日本の伝統技術を継承する職人たちが、建物を安心して使えるように、また建物の本質を後世に確実に伝えられるように熟慮を重ねて行った修復を通して、この文化財は新な価値を得た。中宮寺表御殿は、これからも永い間その優雅な姿を斑鳩の里に保ち続けるのである。

金出ミチル

表御殿外観　修復後
Suite after restoration

Conclusion

On November 30, 2008, an event commemorating the completion of the restoration of the Royal Reception Suite was held at Chūgūji, and the restored building was finally unveiled to those in attendance. During the following few months, the doors of the Royal Reception Suite were opened to allow public viewing of the rooms within this treasured structure for the first time.

After all the restoration procedures had been completed, a new ridge tag was created, recording the period of restoration and the people involved in this project, to be placed in the roof structure. This restoration has added a new chapter to the history of the Suite.

Chūgūji's Royal Reception Suite is an exquisite example of Japanese architectural restoration, in which the preserved masterpiece will convey the work of craftsmen of past and present centuries to future generations. The Suite is now safe, sound, and beautiful, and, it is hoped that for centuries to come it will continue to stand gracefully and with dignity in the Ikaruga district of the ancient capital of Nara.

Michiru Kanade

表御殿修復竣工法要　2008年11月30日
Ceremony for the completion of the Suite's restoration on November 30, 2008

謝　辞

　中宮寺表御殿修復は、中宮寺、日野西光尊門跡の発願で、中宮寺奉賛会名誉総裁三笠宮崇仁親王妃百合子殿下の思召しを賜り、奉賛会会長・中宮寺表御殿修復特別委員会委員長、山口昌紀氏（近畿日本鉄道会長）、中宮寺責任役員、西口廣宗氏（南都銀行会長）、千玄室氏（裏千家大宗匠）、菊池攻氏（奈良トヨタ社長）はじめ、中宮寺信徒総代の方々などのご尽力で日本各地より多くのご支援を賜り、また、ワールド・モニュメント財団の協力により、フリーマン財団、ロバート・ウィルソン財団チャレンジ基金、そしてティファニー財団からの支援でおこなうことができました。
　表御殿修復完成報告法要が2008年11月30日に本堂にて執りおこなわれ、日野西光尊御門跡を導師に、法隆寺管長大野玄妙猊下はじめご一山の奉仕によって、お献茶は裏千家千玄室大宗匠によっておこなわれました。

事業期間：2007年7月〜2008年10月

事業者
設計監理：OFFICE 萬瑠夢　代表　村田信夫
施工業者：社寺建築株式会社 木澤工務店
障壁画工事：株式会社 岡墨光堂

修復専門委員会
特別顧問：鈴木嘉吉、真鍋俊照
専門委員：日向進、澤良雄、山岸常人

表御殿修復プロジェクト協力機関
中世日本研究所（バーバラ・ルーシュ　桂美千代）
ワールド・モニュメント財団（ニューヨーク）
フリーマン財団
ティファニー財団
ロバート・ウィルソン財団チャレンジ基金

写真提供
日野西光尊門跡（p.2, p.12、裏表紙）、村田信夫（p.42-p.68, p.75-p.76、図面含む）、
奈良国立博物館［森村欣司撮影］（p.1, p.5-p.11）、岡墨光堂（p.70-p.75）、
入江泰吉記念奈良市写真美術館（p.18, p.52）、裏千家（p.77）、
渡部巌（表紙、p.12）

出版にあたっては、中宮寺門跡、中宮寺表御殿修復特別委員会、中世日本研究所、及びワールド・モニュメント財団の協力・支援を受けました。

Acknowledgements

The restoration of Chūgūji Imperial Convent in 2008 was planned by Chūgūji Abbess Hinonishi with the great support by Her Imperial Highness Princess Mikasa and made possible by contributors in Japan, with lead support provided by the Chūgūji Restoration Project Committee headed by Mr.Yamaguchi, Chairman of the Board of Kintetsu Corp., Chūgūji Board member, Mr. Nishiguchi, Chairman of the Board of Nanto Bank, Grand tea master Sen Genshitsu and Mr. Kikuchi, President of Nara Toyota Co., Ltd. and other Chūgūji board members.
The restoration was greatly supported by the World Monuments Fund with contributions from the Freeman Foundation, the Robert W. Wilson Challenge to Conserve our Heritage, and The Tiffany & Co. Foundation.
When the restoration of the Royal Reception Suite was completed, Hōryūji abbot and leading monks joined Abbess Hinonishi for a special completion ceremony on November 30, 2008, wherein Tea Master Sen Genshitsu offered tea to Chūgūji's main deity Nyoirin Kannon.

Restoration Project duration: July 2007 to October 2008

Contractors
Project management: Office Marumu, Nobuo Murata
Constructor: Shrine & Temple Construction Kizawa Co.
Painting conservation: Oka Bokkodo Co., Ltd.

Advisory Committee
Special advisor: Kakichi Suzuki, Shunshō Manabe
Committee member: Susumu Hyūga, Yoshio Sawa, Tsuneto Yamagishi

Supporters
Medieval Japanese Studies Institute (Barbara Ruch, Michiyo Katsura)
World Monuments Fund (New York)
Freeman Foundation
The Tiffany & Co. Foundation
Robert W. Wilson Challenge to Conserve our Heritage

Photo credits
Abbess Hinonishi Koson (p.2, p.12, back cover), Nobuo Murata (p.42-p.68, p.75-p.76),
Nara National Museum, Kinji Morimura (p.1, p.5-p.11), Oka Bokkodo (p.70-p.75),
Irie Taikichi Memorial Museum of Photography (p.18, p.52), Urasenke Foundation (p.77),
Iwao Watanabe (cover, p.12)

This book was published cooperatively by Chūgūji Imperial Convent, the Chūgūji Restoration Project Committee, Medieval Japanese Studies Institute and the World Monuments Fund.

中宮寺門跡

2009年4月10日　初版一刷発行

監　修　中宮寺門跡
　　　　636-0111　奈良県生駒郡斑鳩町法隆寺北1-1-2
　　　　phone 0745-75-2106

編　集　中世日本研究所
　　　　　（バーバラ・ルーシュ、桂美千代）
　　　　キャサリン・ルドビック

発行者　浅野泰弘
発行所　光村推古書院株式会社
　　　　603-8115　京都市北区北山通堀川東入
　　　　phone 075-493-8244　fax 075-493-6011
　　　　http://www.mitsumura-suiko.co.jp

印刷・製本　ニューカラー写真印刷株式会社

執筆者プロフィール

キャサリン・ルドビック
トロント大学宗教学博士。インド及び日本宗教専門。京都在住。インドから日本におよぶ女神弁才天の研究を専門とし、大学にて日本の宗教を教える。

Catherine Ludvik, a specialist in Indian and Japanese religion, holds a Ph.D. from the University of Toronto and is a lecturer in Japanese religion based in Kyoto.

金出ミチル
建築修復家。東京大学工学博士。コロンビア大学で歴史保存を学ぶ。各地で建物の調査や修復に関わり、建築保存の裾野を広げることに関心を持つ。

Michiru Kanade, an architectural conservator based in Tokyo, studied historic preservation at Columbia University and holds a Ph.D. in architecture from Tokyo University.

久我なつみ
作家。同志社大学文学部卒業。「日本を愛したティファニー」河出書房新社にて日本エッセイスト・クラブ賞受賞。

Natsumi Kuga, Japan Essayist Club award-winning writer for "Tiffany Who Loved Japan" (available from Kawade Shobo) graduated from Doshisha University.

Chūgūji Imperial Convent

First Edition April 2009

Published by Mitsumura Suiko Shoin Publishing Co., Ltd.

Copyright © 2009 Chūgūji Imperial Convent Printed in Japan

Editors:　Medieval Japanese Studies Institute, Kyoto
　　　　　(Barbara Ruch, Michiyo Katsura)
　　　　　Catherine Ludvik

Publisher:　Yasuhiro Asano

Printer:　New Color Photographic Printing Co., Ltd.

All rights reserved. No part of this book may be reproduced, stored in a retrieval system, or transmitted, in any form or by any means, electronic, mechanical, photocopying, recording or otherwise, without the prior permission of the copyright owners.

ISBN978-4-8381-9972-3